Other books by
BEVERLEY NICHOLS

Novels
EVENSONG
CRAZY PAVEMENTS
PRELUDE
PATCHWORK
SELF

Autobiographies
TWENTY-FIVE
THE STAR SPANGLED MANNER

Essays
ARE THEY THE SAME AT HOME?
WOMEN AND CHILDREN LAST
DOWN THE GARDEN PATH
FOR ADULTS ONLY
CRY HAVOC!

Drama
FAILURES

A
THATCHED ROOF

by
BEVERLEY NICHOLS

illustrated by
REX WHISTLER

· A · THATCHED ·
· ROOF ·

Beverley Nichols

Illustrated by Rex Whistler

JONATHAN CAPE
· LONDON ·

FIRST PUBLISHED 1933
SECOND IMPRESSION, NOVEMBER 1933
THIRD IMPRESSION, DECEMBER 1933

JONATHAN CAPE LTD.   30 BEDFORD SQUARE, LONDON
AND 91 WELLINGTON STREET WEST, TORONTO

PRINTED IN GREAT BRITAIN IN THE CITY OF OXFORD
AT THE ALDEN PRESS
PAPER MADE BY JOHN DICKINSON & CO., LTD.
BOUND BY A. W. BAIN & CO. LTD., IN
CLOTH, FAST TO LIGHT AND WASHABLE,
MADE BY MORTON SUNDOUR FABRICS LTD.

CONTENTS

A PLAGUE ON SEQUELS!

Surely the roses were a deeper red? And the poplars taller? And this path through the borders, which used to be a ribbon threaded through a patchwork of glowing purples—can it have been as tiny as this, as insignificant?

Why is there no music in the wind? Once upon a time, as it sighed through the wood, there was the sound of distant violins — the sweet bow of the wind playing its eternal tunes on the green strings of the trees.

But now there is no music. And even the light seems dim, so that the sundial is mute, and hides Time in a sad shadow.

Why . . . why?

If the sundial could speak it would say:

'Because you were happy in this garden once, and because you are therefore a fool to return to it. All the men who come to ask me the time are fools . . . because they are all looking for something they left behind, and they can never find it. Why — there was a man and a girl only yesterday. They had been in this garden before—a year ago. They had sat under that big yew tree, over there, and her face was as white as the moon, with love, as he kissed it. A year ago! They could tell the time by me then, because the moon was so very bright. It turned my dial to silver and my hour to gold . . . a very tiny hour it was, before they went. But yesterday there was no moon—only a cold wind, which bore the sound of their angry voices to me. They did not come to ask the time, because they stayed only a little while, as they could not find the happiness which they had

9

left behind. It is a pity, because they might have struck a match and read the motto which is engraved on me . . . can you read it yourself?

> *Time as he passes us has a dove's wing,*
> *Unsoiled and swift and of a silken sound.*

'You have read it? You understand? Well, you would be surprised at the number of men who don't. They all try to call the dove back. They call and call, but nearly always the skies remain blank and empty, and the men go away with heavy hearts. It is best that they should go away, for sometimes the dove comes back. It flies haltingly . . . it is tired and wounded . . . and it falls at their feet with crippled wings. That is what happens when men try to recapture some happiness which they have known. . . .'

The light fails . . . 'Without the shadow, Nothing.' And the voice of the sundial fades into a whisper. But I have learnt its lesson. I shall never write a 'sequel.'

§ II

I suddenly realize that a large number of people may not have the least idea what I am talking about. Authors, as a rule, are so apt to over-estimate their own importance that if a few thousand people have read one of their books, they quite forget that a great many millions have not. It may therefore be briefly stated that this book is not a sequel to *Down the Garden Path*. For I hate sequels as much as you do.

The second dodo is never as good as the first. When provincial ladies go further they usually go too far, unless Miss Delafield is conducting them. And I am afraid that even the Forsythes began to outstay their welcome . . . at least, I found myself repeatedly glancing at the clock when they were telling me all about their grandchildren. And so nowadays, whenever the enchanting ladies who work in the book departments of big stores lean towards me with a new novel and say 'you liked his last so much — well, this is a sequel to it. . .' I hurry rapidly away and hide in the millinery department until the danger is past.

For the sundial was right. You should never try to recapture an emotion. The glory has always departed. The sun is never so bright on the hills as you remember it, that week in September, and from another quarter will the wind be blowing.

Therefore this book is not a sequel to an early love; it is rather the other half of the same love. The first book was about a garden; this one is about the cottage which stands in that garden.

Now, while the garden book was being written I constantly found myself longing to take you indoors, for a minute, to show you how the light filtered through the new window which we had knocked out under the eaves, to ask you if you were not excited by the little Sheraton alcove which we discovered, walled up, in the sitting-room, to request that you should peer up the huge chimney, and see how pretty the sky looked at the top, a tiny triangle of blue, in a sooty frame. I wanted to point out to you the wool pictures on the walls . . . in particular, the one which shows Abraham about to sacrifice Isaac, and looking round with an expression of pained surprise at the very fierce angel who is about to tell him to stop such nonsense. I longed to take you upstairs to my bedroom and ask you if anything could possibly be done about it . . . do you think the bed looks too idiotic, for example, with its front feet propped up because the floor is so sloping? And do you think it ought to be raised a foot, so that I could see the top of the laburnum tree when I woke up? Or would it be better to wait till the laburnum grew, and pushed its head in at the window?

Yes . . . all the time I was writing about the garden, I longed to take you in to see the cottage. And now, I suppose, all the time I am writing about the cottage, I shall long to take you into the garden. Yet, it will not be necessary to do so. *For the garden has already come into the cottage.*

Is your house like that? If you are a gardener, I expect it must be. For you can no more stop a garden from walking, in spirit, into the house of a gardener than you can stop the sea from flowing, in spirit, into the house of a sailor.

Who has not known those adorable little houses perched on cliffs, where there is always sand on the floor, a feeling of salt everywhere, a perpetual surge and whisper of waters, and a heavenly scent of ozone? It is like that with my cottage. For there is always a little mud on the floor, a feeling of flowers everywhere, a perpetual surge and whisper of branches, and a heavenly scent of flowers.

In every corner there is evidence of the prevailing passion of its owner. The bottom of nearly every china ornament is black with seeds. There are also seeds in nearly all the cigarette boxes . . . seeds which stick to the cigarettes, and produce a strange smell of burning wool when lit, or even miniature explosions, so that my friends, after one or two experiments, give a sickly smile and say, 'No thanks, really . . . I'd rather have one of my own.'

Every drawer seems to be filled with gardening things. You will probably find pieces of bass and wire on your washstand, several pairs of gardening scissors in the drawer where you want to put your handkerchiefs, and a great many metal tabs on your mantelpiece. The little lobby is always filled with goloshes or gum-boots, and every bookshelf is loaded with catalogues of bulbs, seeds, shrubs and trees. There is usually a pile of bamboo sticks just inside the window, and it is not safe to sit on the sofa till you have made quite certain that there is nothing sharp on it.

There are also little notices, pinned up in odd places all over the house, such as:

TELL S. ABOUT BLIGHT

TELL S. HOSE OUT OF ORDER

COW!

ODD MAN TO LEAVE POND AND DO GRASS

ANTS' NEST

WHAT ABOUT SWEET WILLIAM?

These notices, emerging sharply from the shadows, have been known to disturb my guests, especially the female variety, considerably. To be suddenly confronted with the word cow! when visiting the bath-room for the purposes of improving the face is not the sort of attention they presumably expected. As I am not there (in the bath-room, I mean) I cannot explain that I looked out of the window that morning and saw a peculiarly depraved cow tearing large pieces off my syringa, over the hedge, and wished to remember to take action about it. As for the sweet william, they are apt to take this as a personal question, and exclaim bitterly, that they do not even know anybody called William, and that it is foolish to make bad jokes about it.

But if I go on like this you will be telling me that I am writing a sequel after all: that this book is all about gardening. It really is not . . . it is all about a cottage. And before we begin to argue about it, we had better switch back the clock a few years, shut our eyes, sit on a magic carpet, float across eighty miles of green fields, descend softly in a quiet lane before a rambling old Tudor cottage, in Huntingdonshire, unlatch a tiny gate, push open a green door, and . . .

Bang!

You stagger back, cursing, an agonizing pain in your head.

The cottage, I forgot to tell you, has very low lintels, and I am terribly sorry you have hit your head. So it would really be better if we sat down for a little while. And I will tell you a story.

To
JOHN BORIE
who is still at Allways

A
THATCHED ROOF

CHAPTER I

AS WE WERE

THE low lintels of the cottage have many disadvantages, but they have one supreme advantage. They afford an immediate topic of conversation. They make things start, quite literally, with a bang.

Even the stiffest young guardsman — the type that says, after a long pause, '. . . But my dear fellow, what about India . . . I mean . . . what?' even these young gentlemen find it difficult to concentrate on Imperial problems when they are reeling back from a staggering blow on the forehead.

The lintels are particularly valuable when one is visited by small, arch women who make innuendoes. You know the type. If they belong to the upper classes

they are described in the newspapers as 'petite, with
retroussé features, and, of course, passionately fond of
the open-air.' If they belong to the lower classes they
are described somewhat differently, 'small, snub-nosed
and not much good about the house.'

'Oh! Oh!' they gurgle, as they see their male escorts
rubbing their heads, '*I* can't touch the beams, anywhere
. . . no, I can't . . . not even if I stand on tiptoe!'
There is then a great deal of fluttering and gesturing in
various corners to make sure that they cannot touch the
beams. After which they twist round and say, 'Why it
must have been *built* for me, don't you think?' A high
laugh and a slight roll of the eye. They tiptoe up . . .
'Did you *ever* have anybody as tiny as me in the cottage
before?'

To which the unspoken answer is, 'Yes . . . I am afraid
I have had lots of people as tiny as you . . . and one
day one of them will be squashed. . . .' Actually I
smile and ask if they have noticed the bunches of flowers
which are pinned to the beams.

These flowers are pinned up all over the house, as
danger signals. The idea is that just before you go
through a low door, or under a very sloping part of the
ceiling, you will catch sight of the flowers and bend down.

Most people do not seem to notice them, and go on
banging their heads with undiminished energy. But I
keep the flowers there because they are so pretty. There
is a bunch of very bright everlasting flowers right in the
centre of the garden room ceiling. When the sun shines
on it, the flowers glow like little lamps of gold and ruby.
There is a bunch of lavender over the doorway . . . a
beautiful bunch that you can sniff as you go in to dinner.

There are dried beech leaves and berries, very carefully and tidily arranged . . . and very charming they look against the sombre black beams, though you might not believe it. It need hardly be said that there are never any fresh flowers. When I see a cut flower out of water, I feel thirsty until the poor thing has had a drink.

The low ceilings are most valuable of all for a particular type of person whom I really adore, the type that can always be relied upon to deliver exactly the right platitude at the right moment. You must know her . . . (the type flourishes a little less freely in the male variety). For example —

When your dog curls round and round on the hearthrug, before settling down, she says:

'I always think it's *so* interesting when dogs do that, don't you? They say it comes from the time when they were wild, you know—doesn't it? When they were in the desert . . . and had to make a place for themselves in the long grass.'

This lady is the mistress of a multitude of clichés which begin with 'I always think.' When she enters the study she says, 'I always think books furnish a room, don't you?' When she walks round the rose beds in late September she says 'I always think the second crop is better than the first, don't you?' However, this book would never begin if we were to make a catalogue of all her pleasant, homespun sayings, so we must be content to chronicle her remark about the low ceilings, which is:

'I always think people must have been much *shorter* when these cottages were built, don't you?'

'I wonder.'

And, indeed, I do wonder. That platitude sets free

a flock of dreams. The cottage was built about 1540. Four centuries ago. A lot can happen in four centuries. And before we know where we are, our minds have flown back . . . back . . . and it is spring, and that sweet monster Henry VIII is on the throne. But the village of Allways is standing, white and fair in the early morning, and the flowers in the cottage gardens are much the same. The wallflowers as gay, the forget-me-nots a little smaller perhaps, but no less true a blue.

This is terrible. Four centuries ago! When all we have to worry about is a little matter of four years!

§ 11

It was four years ago that I bought my cottage. I bought it lock, stock and barrel, as it stood . . . with all the furniture, carpets, pictures, pots, and pans.

At least, that was what I thought.

The cottage had belonged to a very charming American, who shared it with an old musician. I had only seen it once before, but I had fallen in love at first sight. I remembered a winding lane in a remote part of England's second smallest county . . . white heavily-timbered walls . . . a sloping thatch . . . and long low rooms, furnished with the utmost simplicity.

The American died. The old musician followed him. And I bought the cottage.

Now, of course, you should be introduced to the various rooms straight away, instead of being kept standing about, or made to wander down odd corridors. But I fear that in all this book we shall be wandering into odd corridors — seeing a gleam of light through an

old window — going up to it to note how gaily it illu-
minates the old maps of Huntingdon on the wall,
limning some faded field with a passing radiance. So
you must forgive me if I say a word about the American,
for he was a fine man . . . quiet and wise, with an eye
in which the green things of the world were always
brightly mirrored. And he is buried in the little church-
yard of Allways.

On his grave are the words:

AN AMERICAN WHO LOVED ENGLAND

Round the grave there is a thick band of glossy ivy,
which I planted three years ago. You may think it
strange to plant ivy round a man's grave, but this ivy
came from Long Island, so it seemed a little more appro-
priate. When I was in America, living on the thirtieth
story of an apartment house, I hungered for the sight of
something green outside my window. And so, one day
when I was visiting Long Island I begged a pot of this
ivy, took it back, and placed it outside the window, where
it flourished exceedingly, putting out its pert green
leaves high above the roaring traffic.

When I left America I threw the ivy, pot and all, into
an old coal-scuttle. It was packed with the rest of the
furniture, and stored for months, during which time I
am ashamed to say that I forgot all about it. However,
when at last I found a house, and unstored the furniture,
there was the ivy . . . still living, after six months
without light or water, in an old packing-case! I remember it so well, as we lifted out the coal-scuttle and
brushed the straw away. There was one pale shoot at
the end of an almost brittle branch — a shoot so pale

that it was like the waxy complexion of one dead. But no, the ivy was alive. I took it out, ran downstairs with it as though every minute was precious, watered it gently, and set it on a table in the back yard, sheltered from even the dim silver sun of London. From that moment it has never 'looked back.'

§III

On and on we wander in these pages — and we never reach the point because, happily, there is no point to reach. So I feel at liberty to ask you a question.

Have you this same odd affection for things, like my ivy, which show tremendous courage in the face of adversity? For plants, and animals, and people, even if they are common plants, and worthless animals and dull people? It may be a purely personal weakness, but I feel that somewhere there must be some one who shares it with me. Often, in the garden, I have found some plant that has seeded itself in a spot where you would think its frail roots could not possibly gain a hold. Perhaps it is only a common rock-plant that has pitched its gay camp on some wind-swept, barren wall, and is flying its yellow flag in the teeth of every wind. But though it is 'common,' the miraculous courage of such a plant defeats me. I could no more destroy it even if it is an intruder, than I could tear up a rose tree that was decked in all the crimson regalia of July.

It is the same with animals. I hate spiders, but if a spider has woven an elaborate web in some room where no flies come, if it has flung this tenuous fabric across the deserted airs, with God knows what optimism, I hesitate to destroy it. (I need hardly say that I destroy with great pleasure, and the utmost sadism, the webs of those fat brown spiders which are hung out, like sinister laundry lines, on summer mornings when the flies are abundant.) As for other animals — for dogs that ought to have died, and the kitten that ought to have been drowned but was overlooked — however that subject would lead us too far astray, even in so desultory a promenade as we are making.

To return to the ivy. After a few days in the open air, with plenty of water, and a great many kind words, the colour began to come back into the solitary leaf, and soon another leaf formed, and yet another, until after a few weeks I felt that it was strong enough to stand the journey, and I took it up to Allways. There were two roots of it, and I planted them side by side, calling one of them 'Hoover' and the other 'Al Smith.' A race ensued, up the wall, in which Al Smith, to my great delight, was an easy winner — and still is. When I planted the ivy on the grave I took a cutting from both plants, because I knew that if the American had been there, he would have smiled at this little idea. And now, under the shadow of the yew tree, Al Smith and Hoover have mingled together, so that you cannot tell their leaves apart. . . .

§ I V

In a moment we will enter the hall and make the tour of the rooms, one by one. But first there is an explanation to be made.

As I have said before, I bought the cottage lock, stock

and barrel. However, it was nearly a year before I could return from America to occupy it, or even to visit it. And in the meantime there was an interregnum, when it was let to some very rich people whom we will call the Montagues.

The idea was that the Montagues were to leave the cottage in the state in which they found it. After a somewhat protracted experience, I have come to the conclusion that nobody ever leaves anything (or anybody) in the state in which he found it. However, in those days, I was innocent. And when the Montagues wrote, from time to time, and dropped mysterious little hints about 'improvements—of which we are sure you will approve' and soft suggestions that 'we have some rather charming pieces that we would like to leave — as a memento, you know . . .' (pieces of what, I wondered?) and again — 'the walls of the garden-room were terribly shabby, so we have had them done up . . . I'm sure you will adore the shade . . .' I only thought how nice the Montagues were, and how lucky I was to be getting all these beautiful things for nothing.

Then I returned to England. There came a day in March when the Montagues departed. I waited a couple of days till Arthur, the servant engaged by the solicitors, had settled in. And then I went up. I went up by train, and sat all alone, very haughtily, in a first-class carriage, because I felt I could not bear to share this great moment with anybody.

It was a bitterly cold afternoon in early March. The swiftly passing landscape had been etched with a frozen pen. The boughs of the ashes were black against a sky of steel; the rolling fields of pasture land were deserted,

save for a few sheep that huddled near the threadbare
hedges. Black and grey it all was, but I was warm
because my heart was beating high with the spirit of
adventure.

'There will be a fire,' I said to myself. 'My own fire.
I have never had my own fire before — it has really
always belonged to somebody else. But this will be my
grate — and the earth beneath the grate will belong to
me and the sky above. And when the smoke drifts up,
dancing to the stars that hang, like golden fruit, just
above my eaves, the smoke will still be mine because it
will come from my own logs.'

And I fell to wondering if it would feel very terrible to
burn one's own logs, or if the excitement of it would make
up for the feeling that a tree had died? If it was a
favourite tree, surely one could never burn it? To burn a
branch which has whispered to you on summer nights
— which has sheltered you, which you have caressed
. . . no, that would be impossible. Besides — it is much
more fun to climb the hedge that leads to your neigh-
bours' fields, and creep round at dusk, to the old ash that
was blown down last March, and gather a great bundle
of wood which doesn't belong to you.

But let us skip these dreams; let us bustle into the
village Ford which is waiting at the station, drive through
three miles of wintry lanes, alight at a white rambling
cottage, open the latch with trembling fingers, hurry
through the tiny hall, and stand in the doorway of the
Garden Room, as I stood four years ago, looking at . . .
at what?

CHAPTER II

SCENE-SHIFTING

My first impression was one of intense cold. The lamps had not yet been lit, and the room was grey and cheerless. Nor was there any fire — instead, a peculiarly hideous oil-stove was making hot local smells in a corner. At least, the heat was local. The smell was omnipresent.

But it was not only the absence of fire which made me shiver. What was it? I stared around me. What had happened to the room I remembered and loved — the warm, simple room with the white walls and the gay pattern of old oak beams? Beams! That was it! They had all been covered up!

I took a step forward. I peered at the wall. Yes — there they were — there was the mark of the wood. But it was all covered over with a yellow distemper. Lord — that yellow — it makes me feel jaundiced to this day.

I ran my fingers up and down the wall. It was enough to make one weep. But there was no time for weeping. There was too much in the room which made me angry.

There was, for example, one of those open cupboards which are known as Welsh dressers, filled with fake pewter. I have no objection to Welsh dressers — though I should never go out of my way to deprive the Welsh of them. But when they are made of fake olde oake, and carved over the top with the sickly words 'Easte is

Easte, Weste is Weste, Home is Beste' . . . then I feel
singularly little affection for the Welsh. The word home,
I may add, was spelt 'hame', to give a Scottish touch.

I glowered at it. Tried to stare it out of countenance.
But it outstared me, with all its arrogant pewter eyes.
There was a road-house atmosphere about it. You know
the sort of road-house I mean. It lies about twenty miles
out of London, and is exactly six months old. There is
always a terrifically Tudor swimming pool in the garden,
which is illuminated at night with olde lanternes. There
is also an American bar which is so Tudor that they
never have any ice for the cocktails, and a highly Tudor
radio set which the barmaid turns on with her tapering
Tudor fingers. Fiendish young men in plus-fours emerge
from small vociferous cars at all times of the day and
night and make jokes that fall with such weight that one
wonders why the Olde Tudor floor does not crack
beneath the strain. And all the time the Welsh dresser
glimmers in the background with its load of fake pewter
thoroughly at home, enjoying itself.

Well — that was the thing which the Montagues had
placed in my Garden Room as the *pièce de résistance!*
And all over the house it was the same. There were fake
samplers stuck up on the wall, fake warming-pans, fake
grandfather clocks. There were disgusting little bags of
potpourri in the drawers — the sort of potpourri that
smells like cabbage scented with Chypre. There were
positively frightening candles in the fake Tudor candlesticks, candles that were tinted mauve and had gold
drops trickling down them — the sort of candles which,
I hope, will light their manufacturers to hell.

Enough of this. We will end in my bedroom. This

29

room, I hoped, might have been spared. It had been
monastically simple, as I remembered it. Bare boards,
a plain white bedstead, a single wheel-back chair and a
table with a Queen Anne mirror on it.

Ye gods! When I opened the door, I saw another
Welsh dresser! Even Welsher and dressier than the one
downstairs. And the walls had come out in a rash of
samplers, warming-pans and Lord knows what else!

But the worst thing of all was spread on the bed itself.

No . . . it was not Mrs. Montague, though I should not
have been in the least surprised to see her there, swathed
in Tudor tulle, burbling that Easte might be Easte and
Weste might be Weste but *Hame* — (here, a deep sigh
into the tulle) — was undoubtedly Beste.

Mrs. Montague, luckily for her, was not lying on my
bed at that moment. Something even worse was there.
A synthetic patchwork. A patchwork that was obviously,
in some subtle way, related to the Welsh dresser. A
printed patchwork, that had been turned out by the
hundred thousand.

Now I happen to have rather a feeling about patchwork. Real patchwork, I mean. I am the proud posses-
sor of one which was made for me by an old lady of
eighty — the prettiest old lady you ever saw, whose eyes
are still as blue as pimpernels. This patchwork is an
intoxicating fabric, for it is made of hundreds of dia-
mond-shaped fragments of silk and brocade — little
bits of old Court dresses, squares of printed velvet, tiny
patches of gold-threaded satin. If you bend over it you
lose yourself in an enchanted domain — your eyes stray
from a piece of silk that has one tiny silver rose in the
centre to a black velvet that is boldly spotted with

emerald, to a cretonne with a spray of yellow leaves. And you fall to wondering who were the women who wore the dresses from which these lovely fragments were taken, through what halls these satins have swept, to what soft tunes the silks have drifted. Oh, to be able to wave a magic wand, to send each tiny piece flying back, over the years, to follow, and to listen! Into what glittering chambers would one be led . . . and what secrets one would hear, in long corridors where the silk sounded like a caress, and in the deep shadows of summer gardens, when the fountains were playing!

Yes — you will agree — a patchwork is a pretty thing. And that is why I resented so bitterly the monstrous parody of a patchwork that was reposing on my bed. For it was printed, on cheap satin, and it came from Minneapolis. It was about as hideous a conception as has ever emerged from the mind of man. In the centre of it, on a square of white satin, was stamped a nauseating reproduction of a Tudor cottage, with rather blurred smoke drifting up into a cheap blank sky. And under the cottage was once more that dread inscription — 'Easte is Easte, Weste is Weste, Hame is Beste.'

I averted my eyes. I held my nose. I stepped towards the bed, plucked the offensive thing between the thumb and forefinger of my right hand, opened the window, and dropped it outside. It caught on a branch of wistaria. I let it hang there. I noted, with relief, that it was beginning to rain, so that some of the horrible colours would be washed away. I had a momentary fear that the dyes might be poisonous, and would kill the wistaria. I decided to risk it, rather than touch the thing again.

I stared out of the window, resting my chin on my

hands. It was quite dark now, and very still and cold.
I stared and stared at the night sky, whose violet curtains
were thickly hung with stars. And as I stared it seemed
that even the stars began to arrange themselves into
Gothic letters, spelling the Montague slogan — 'Easte
is Easte . . .'

§ 11

There now ensued a series of extremely acid telegrams.
When you send a telegram at Allways you have to walk
across a field, go down a lane to the post office, and hand
your telegram to one of the charming daughters of the
postmistress, who then proceeds to telephone it to the
next exchange. I think that a lot of rooks have made
their nests in the wires between Allways, because there is
always a noise of cawing and buzzing, so that she often
has to repeat the message several times, in a very loud
voice, to the great elevation and delight of any village
boys who may be buying stamps at the time. I fear she
grew tired of repeating some of those early telegrams.
They ran something like this:

Mrs Montague —— Hotel London
Kindly remove all your furniture at once
Nichols

Nichols Allways Huntingdonshire
You were fully informed of all improvements and
additions and agreed to keep furniture we estimate
value at two hundred pounds cheque would oblige
Montague

Mrs Montague —— Hotel London
I estimate damages two hundred guineas kindly
send cheque and van to-morrow   Nichols

Nichols Allways Huntingdonshire
Our solicitor will call on you to-morrow arriving
eleven-thirty   Montague

Mrs Montague —— Hotel London
Kindly tell solicitor shall claim another fifty guineas
for moral and æsthetic shock caused by your settee.
                                                  Nichols

And thus, and thus. On the next day the solicitor
arrived. He proved a charming man, of exquisite taste.
He helped me to drape some of the more offensive objects
with dust sheets.

He told me that I should hear no more about the
matter, and he drew up a letter to the Montagues, which
I signed, informing them that I proposed to remove all
their belongings at the earliest opportunity. He added
a postscript, which I initialled, saying that I would not
charge them anything for dilapidations.

Oh yes — he was a clever man that solicitor. I believe
I could have got a lot of money out of the Montagues.
But I was so happy to be rid of them that I didn't care.

§ III

Two days later the van arrived, to remove all traces of
the Montague regime.

Anybody who has ever suffered the ordeal of moving
house will agree with me that even the best of one's

furniture, when brought into the daylight, looks frightful. Chairs that seemed quite handsome are suddenly
shown to be cracked all over, as though they had been
hurled round the room, and sofas that had appeared
impeccable are revealed as having the stuffing coming
out of them, as though they had been bitten in unspeakable orgies. Screens look faded and shabby, pictures
appear insignificant and faintly ridiculous. As for
photographs of friends and relations — which are
always chosen by the furniture men to be leant against
the wall, outside the front door, these look monstrously
absurd. The dogs come and sniff them, with dubious
expressions, the street boys come and stare at them, and
you long to go up and say 'Really, she isn't quite as
plain as that . . .' or 'You mayn't believe it, but she *is*
a lady.'

However, when the furniture is not one's own but
somebody else's, and when it is of so wildly embarrassing
a nature as the Montagues', the agony is greatly intensi-
fied. Especially when the removal is carried out in so
glaring a light of publicity.

Publicity — you say? How can there be any publicity about a furniture removal in a country lane? Well,
my experience has been that if you try to do anything —
yes *anything* — in a country lane, you seldom get away
with it. Perhaps we might have been safe if the men
had come in the dead of night, as I tried to persuade
them to do, but instead they came on one of April's
most brilliant days — a day as sparkling as a newly-
washed lemon . . . a day when even the shadows were
a melange of blue and orange and jade, like the shadows
that poured from the tipsy brush of Monet.

'The men have come,' announced Mrs. Wrench, as I was having breakfast. (Mrs. Wrench, of whom you will hear more later, was the housekeeper who had superseded the sinister Arthur. She was heavily built, mournful and a windy cave of sighs.)

I looked up. What a day, I thought, as I noticed how Monet Mrs. Wrench's face had become! There was a mauve diamond under her chin, and her dress was slashed with orange as the tigerish sunlight leapt through the window. A pool of gold was the floor and the ceiling laughed and leaped with a largesse of silver. Shadows here, shadows there, and all the shadows were tinted — there were even pinks and purples on the window panes, like bubbles newly-blown. Oh, the freshness of that April day . . . the enchantment of it . . . when the earth itself was a bubble . . . drunkenly spun through space, with the liquid shades of the rainbow caressing it . . .

'Yes, Mrs. Wrench.'

'The men have come.'

I stared at my egg. Orange and white . . . a lovely design. Stop this nonsense, I said to myself.

'Oh yes.' I got up. 'Which room do they want to clean out first?'

'It's immaterial to me, sir.'

'Then they'd better begin upstairs.'

Let us now skip three hours.

It is midday. The sunlight is so dazzling that one feels the tiniest beetle must be creeping desperately into the remotest shadow he can find, lest he get sunstroke.

On the little lawn in front of my cottage is ranged the Montague collection of monstrosities. The Welsh dressers of course are displayed in a place of honour, so are the Tudor candlesticks. Apart from these there are painted tables. . . chipped commodes . . . (that are utterly incommodious) . . . frightful little statuettes, staring on to the hedges with eyes like bad grapes . . . ornaments . . . bric-à-brac . . . a revolting collection.

For hours, I had been hurrying backwards and forwards, asking the men why the things could not be put in the van instead of being left on the lawn. To this I received no satisfactory reply. They had first to 'see what there was,' they said. It was useless to point out to them that it was only too easy to see what there was . . . because what there was was the sort of thing that would bark at you on a dark night. They paid no attention. And meanwhile the crowd outside increased.

For the whole village had become aware that something was astir at my cottage, and there was a perpetual lingering procession of onlookers. When I was on the lawn, the members of the procession kept up an outward show of aloofness, stuck their hands in their pockets and strolled away a few yards, or retired to the hedge, and pretended to be very interested in the brambles. But the minute I retired into the house they gathered together again, gazing with a sort of hideous mockery at the Montague monstrosities.

§IV

As ill-luck would have it, the very first object to be moved was a large china statuette of a negress clasping to her bosom a somewhat startled lamb. What this peculiar conjunction was intended to convey, morally or æsthetically, I do not know. There was a little brass plaque at the bottom of the statuette bearing the cryptic title:

'The Black Sheep. Walter MacAdams,
Philadelphia 1892.'

What could this mean? The sheep was not black. It was white. Had it, perhaps, misbehaved? Or was the negress the offender, and was she obtaining comfort from the sheep? Or had they both misbehaved? It was really very confusing. One was forced to the conclusion that it was intended to convey some very moral lesson, about negresses and sheep being all the same in the eyes of God, or something equally embarrassing.

This object greatly appealed to the village boys. What was the something lady doing with the something sheep, they demanded; and why the something had the sheep got such a something tail? Something told me that if I did not go out and freeze them with my presence, there would be a riot. So I went out.

The village boys melted away, to a discreet distance. But down the road came Mrs. M.

Now we shall be seeing quite a lot of Mrs. M. during our pilgrimage together, so we had better see her clearly. It is enough that you should visualize a tall, wiry woman of about forty, brimming with energy, somewhat hatchet-faced, with rabbit's teeth. She has many admirable qualities. She runs her charming house, at the other end of the village, with the utmost efficiency. Her tables are more highly polished, her garden more damnably prolific, her 'little dinners' more delicious, than any other woman's in Huntingdonshire. But she has two great drawbacks. She is utterly devoid of humour. And she always arrives at the wrong moment.

'Ha!' she cried, in tones of the utmost penetration. 'Spring-cleaning all your household gods?'

I groaned in spirit. I could not shout as loudly as Mrs. M. to tell the village boys that these were *not* my household gods, and that I was *not* spring-cleaning them, but sending them far, far away. One would have had a sore throat before one was able to convey to those vacant, watching faces even a quarter of this information.

So I merely gave a sickly smile.

It was difficult to smile. For I was dismayed and dejected by the thought that the village boys would imagine that I *liked* something negresses clasping something sheep. They would attribute this morbid and utterly Philadelphian taste to me. Whenever they saw a sheep they would think of negresses, and heaven knows what complications would ensue. And as I had to live in the village I did want to keep the village fairly sane.

'One's things never look their best in the open air, do they?' she boomed.

'These aren't my things. They're the Montagues'. And I think they're all too frightful. So they're going away.'

'Oh!' Mrs. M. suddenly noticed The Black Sheep. She hastily averted her eye, as though afraid that if she examined it more closely she might see something that was not *quite* . . . However she is a woman who can never be embarrassed for more than a few seconds. She said:

'If you're sending all these things away, what are you going to do for furniture?'

'I shall get it gradually.'

'But what about blankets, and linen, and all your kitchen things?' This question was prompted by one of the removal men who staggered past, at that moment, laden with a bundle of mauve blankets — (I swear they were mauve) — and Tudor warming-pans.

'I'm getting all those at once.'

Mrs. M. licked her lips at this opportunity to give advice to a poor benighted bachelor. I also (mentally) licked my lips at the opportunity to refuse to accept such advice.

'But have you any system?' She pronounced the word 'system' with that sort of hiss which, I have noticed, is always employed by women when talking of household matters — as though domestic affairs were strange and secret mysteries, which only women could understand.

'Well, it's all quite simple, isn't it?'

'Simple!' Mrs. M. said the word with horror, as though I had uttered a hideous blasphemy against the sacred mysteries of the household gods. And indeed, I had. For if you dare to suggest to a woman that running a house is a simple matter, you are regarded as though you were a profane and perverted creature who had broken into some temple and tried to tear the veil from the eyes of the high priest.

'Simple!' echoed Mrs. M. She made a gesture with her hands — a gesture of despair. I could see that she was preparing to deliver a homily on the hopelessness of Man when confronted with these problems.

'You've no *idea*,' she said, 'the number of things you'll want.'

'But I have a very clear idea indeed,' I said, somewhat tersely. 'I've written them all down on this piece of paper.' And I waved a little sheet of note-paper I happened to be carrying.

'What? On that?' Mrs. M. glared at it, trying to see what was written on it. (The only words I had written were 'Order gin.') 'You couldn't possibly get all you want on there.'

'I could, Mrs. M., and I have. I want very little. And I write very small.'

'What about dusters, and dish-cloths, and saucepans and brushes?'

'They are all on this little sheet of paper,' I said, 'even down to the thing with holes in it that you use for lifting out the fish.' And I returned the piece of paper to my pocket.

'Well, I must say it would be a miracle if any *man* ordered everything a woman wants for the house.' Mrs. M.'s eyes strayed hungrily towards my pocket. 'I wouldn't mind betting there are fifty things on that list you've forgotten.'

'I don't think there are, Mrs. M.'

'Well . . .,' said Mrs. M. She licked her lips again and breathed very heavily. 'Well!' And so, as one cannot go on saying 'well' for very long, without encouragement, especially when furniture removers are assiduously carrying china negresses under one's nose, she gave it up, and departed.

I watched her striding down the lane. She was swing-ing her stick with quite unnecessary violence, and speaking very harshly to her super-aristocratic terrier, which has legs as straight as ramrods, and a morbidly twitching nose. And I knew — oh, how well I knew — that Mrs. M. was waiting for the day when she would be asked to lunch, in order that she might note that the fish was broken, because I had been lying about the thing with holes in it, and that the napkins didn't match, because I had forgotten to get new ones.

Well, Mrs. M. has been to lunch with me on many occasions since that dazzling April morning. And really, she has never found anything very vital to complain about.

§ v

You see, I began my household economy on the masculine principle of waiting for things to turn up. There is a really vital distinction between this and the feminine principle of turning things up without waiting.

In other words, for a brief space we 'did'. If anything was missing, we ordered it as the occasion arose. That seems to me to be really the best way of doing things. It is the man's way, rather than the woman's way, but honestly it seems to me to be the best way. A woman might have been more methodical, and in some ways more economical, but I am quite certain that she would have littered up her kitchen and her pantry with all sorts of unnecessary objects. I have never seen a hundred per cent feminine kitchen, for example, which does not contain at least three of those hideous whirring machines that are used for beating up eggs. When the eggs are beaten up, they are invariably used to create a disgusting sort of sweet in which a loathsome cloud of hot white of egg hovers over a brooding mass of raspberry jam and sponge-cake. Such instruments of torture are absent from my kitchen for the simple reason that I have never felt any great urge to devour such diabolical dishes.

Again I have never seen a hundred per cent feminine kitchen which is not stocked with quantities of highly enamelled tins, deceitfully stamped, on the outside, with the names of commodities which they never contain. There is, for example, a tin labelled RICE, which invariably contains a ball of string and a photograph of the cook's fiancé. There is also a tin labelled TEA, which holds anything from cocoa to sultanas. And always there is a tin labelled with the terrible word SAGO. I have never opened this tin for fear I should actually find sago lurking inside it, like a fiendish jellyfish, which would be more than I could bear.

Such cheating symbols are absent from my kitchen. On the other hand, there are a great many things which are usually absent from the hundred per cent feminine kitchen. There are, for example, at least a dozen corkscrews, instead of the solitary corkscrew which women consider sufficient — a corkscrew which is usually kept concealed in the knife-drawer behind a lot of old dusters. There are also quantities of matches. And in the larder there are rows of tongues and bottled chickens and all the things one wants when one feels like raiding the larder at midnight.

However we must not linger in the kitchen. There are too many exciting things going on in the other parts of the cottage.

The
Garden Room

CHAPTER III

WHITE BEAUTY

A FEW weeks elapse. The scene-shifters have departed and the stage is almost bare. A few essential pieces remain, dotted about the cottage — a bed here, a chair there, a table or two. But the general feeling is one of emptiness. I tiptoe through it, listening to the echoes.

Anybody who has ever owned an empty cottage will agree that emptiness can be very exciting. Lank, neglected hollyhocks look in through the window, and undisciplined spiders among the beams weave webs of fantastic delicacy, as though they imagine that this regime is going on for ever. The light lingers in pools of gold on the old brick floors, and is only reluctantly swept up by the black broom of night. There is great mystery in this emptiness, and the silence is stranger here than in the wide spaces outside — for in the garden, even on the stillest days, one can always hear a faint break of leafy surf from the green shores of the forest. But in the cottage there is only a sigh, now and then, and a tiny creak from the old beams, as though they were weary of stretching their black arms across the ceiling, century after century.

It is difficult to disturb this emptiness. It is as though one were trying to shout in a cathedral. But it has to be done. And I think the best way to set about it is to go to the principal room in the house, lock the door, sit on a packing-case, smoke a cigarette, and decide what the foundations are to be.

45

Now the principal room in my cottage is the Garden Room, in the front of the cottage. It has seven windows and is as completely surrounded by the garden as an island is surrounded by sea. I suppose I ought to describe this room in detail. But descriptions of rooms, in books, are almost as boring as descriptions of faces, and quite as useless. Who has not groaned, inwardly, when reading a novelist's long description of his heroine's features?

'Her mouth, perhaps, was a trifle too large . . .' (her mouth is *always* a trifle too large in all the best novels, which arouses the gloomiest suspicions as to the tastes of the average novelist) . . . 'and her nose had a faint upward tilt. Her eyes were her most striking character-istic.' (They always are.) 'And though not strictly beautiful' etc. etc. The net result of all this is that the reader gathers that Mr. Smith, the novelist, likes large-mouthed, turn-up-nosey women, who are not 'strictly' beautiful. Nor 'strictly' anything else, judging by the way they go on in the last few chapters.

It is the same with rooms. Unless the man is the Dickens of a genius, his loftiest descriptions help you less than an auctioneer's inventory. And so all I shall say about the Garden Room, where the adventure really began, is that it is large and squarish, with low ceilings and a feeling of sunlight dancing over floors of old red brick, through the seven windows.

§ I I

I sat in the Garden Room, in the beginning of things, with the door locked, and the smoke from my cigarette drifting through the empty airs. And it was all terrible, because the walls were distempered a sickly lemon colour and the beams were painted over, and the floors were covered with that dreadful linoleum which pretends to be parquet flooring and looks like the symptoms of the worst sort of disease. So terrible was this room, in fact, that it made me feel positively unclean. It made me long for something very cool, and very simple. And it drove me to white in sheer desperation.

The Garden Room was the first room which was white-washed, but the result was so triumphant that now every inch of my cottage is white — the pure white of snow and lilies.

Of course it is late in the day to sing the praises of White — to proclaim the fact that of all backgrounds it is the most restful, the most friendly, and the happiest to live with. For about two years ago 'Society' discovered white, and since then it has been done to death. There have been endless white parties, in which the women looked like glistening china ornaments and danced before banks of lilies on which the light shone through vases of alabaster. There have been all-white weddings, in which the best man wore a stock of white satin that reached to his stomach and the church was knee-deep in camellias, white carnations, and Ophelia roses. There have been white fêtes, and white pageants and white parades, and one young woman of my acquaintance, on her father's death, was bitterly disappointed because her mother would not consent to an all-white funeral.

'*Dead* white, sir?' said Mr. Joy, rather doubtfully, when I told him what I wanted. Mr. Joy is the local plasterer and undertaker. His wife keeps the village shop, and very well she keeps it too.

47

'Yes, as white as you can get it.'

'Won't that be a little cold, sir? Wouldn't you like a little dash of cream . . . to give you body?'

I intimated to Mr. Joy that I should very much dislike a little dash of cream to give me body. I had quite enough body as it is, without any little dashes of cream. And I reflected on the strange ways of decorators, who, as a class, are invariably so hostile to their clients' suggestions. White is a comparatively easy matter, because if you go on saying 'white, white, white,' against all recommendations of cream and body, you will eventually get white. But when it comes to green . . . there one despairs. The only thing to do is to mix the paints oneself. It is no use pointing to those frightful little cards of colours which the painters always show you, and saying 'I want that one.' You will never get it. The colour on the card bears not the least resemblance to the colour which will eventually sneer at you from the wall. No — if you want green you must mix it yourself. And I am sure you want the same green as I want, which is the colour of young grass, fresh and living and natural, with no trace of blue, and no suggestion of the chemist's shop.

Anyway we got white, at last.

And now we can return to the Garden Room. It is high summer, and the sun is a perpetual beneficence from dawn till dusk. It dances far more freely now — up and down, in and out, in every shade of gold, playing lovely melodies of colour on its white keyboard, with the black notes of the beams sounding sonorously through the whole enchanted rhythm.

The foundations are laid. And now, the first discovery is made.

§III

I was in the Garden Room one morning, rejoicing in the whiteness and the sunlight, and the emptiness. I was lazily weaving patterns in my head of the room which was to be, patterns of curtains, and coloured glasses, and deep chintz chairs. And then I happened to lean rather heavily against the wall . . . and the wall sounded hollow.

It was in a corner between the window and the fireplace. There was no sort of reason why the wall should be hollow here. At first I thought I must be mistaken.

I stepped back -- looked at the wall, stretched out my hand and tapped, very gently.

Echoes!

Tapped again, with a heart that beat swiftly.

Echoes again! Only tiny echoes. Reluctant, faint, and halting, as though summoned from dim and distant corridors — where they had thought themselves safe from the clamour of life.

It seemed almost cruel to disturb those echoes. They had slept for so long. The deep coverlet of time had been drawn so surely over them — their sleep had seemed so secure — they had forgotten the loud sunlight, and the silly birds, and the tramp of men.

Yet, I had to disturb them. I couldn't help it. An empty room — a hollow wall — one just can't leave these things to rest. That is one of the damnable characteristics of man. And so, with vulgar excitement, I rapped and rapped, assured myself that I was not mistaken, ran across the room, flung open the door, and shouted:

D   49

'Mr. Joy . . . Mr. Joy.'

With dreadful slowness Mr. Joy descended. He lumbered into the room, saw the blank space, tapped it, said it certainly sounded hollow, but it would make a fine mess to open it . . . yielded to argument, fetched his tools, struck the new, glistening steel into the old wood.

I closed my eyes.

There was a rending, a dust of plaster, and then, at last, the boards came away, clattered to the floor, and it was revealed.

'It' was a perfect Sheraton alcove, painted a faded white, with five shelves, and a very delicately carved shell poised in a tiny ribbed ceiling. The whole alcove was no bigger than a man standing upright, but its design was exquisite. Its date, I should say, was about 1780.

However, this was not the main excitement. For on the centre of the alcove stood a lady in a white dress. She was a Staffordshire lady with a white hat, and white arms, and the only colour about her was in the green china grass at her feet and the pale yellow sheaf of corn under her arm. Even her lips were white, and so were her eyes, which stared out at us with a curious calm, as though she were not at all surprised at being wakened from her sleep of so many years.

'Well I never . . .' said Mr. Joy.

'How did that alcove get there?'

Mr. Joy shook his head. He did not know. And indeed, it was a mystery. For until the American had the cottage — (and the American would certainly never have entombed a lovely white lady in a perfect Sheraton alcove) — the cottage had belonged to three poor families.

For centuries, so the legend ran, it had been inhabited by farm labourers, ploughboys and other charming men who work with their bodies. These were certainly not the people to go to the expense of building a Sheraton alcove into a Tudor cottage — and it obviously *had* been built in — nor would they be either so foolish or so unkind as to shut up such a pretty lady in it.

The mystery deepened the more one thought about it. And many strange fancies fluttered in and out of that cupboard, with white and aerie wings — of how there had once been a Lord of the Manor who had loved a village girl, and betrayed her — how he turned her parents out of the cottage and made wild love to the frightened girl on stormy nights, when the wind whistled through the tattered rigging of the elms. How there was a quarrel and angry words, and how, suddenly, she was lying there on the floor, in the white moonlight of the eighteenth century, lying so still that even the elms were hushed. And the wicked Earl — for he was obviously an earl — had her body taken away, and caused a starving genius to make a model of her, which he set in this lovely alcove. Then he walled her up, and locked the door, and stole away, chuckling, under the elms.

You will agree that there is substance there for plenty of dreams. But we have no time for dreams. There are too many facts, waiting to be told.

§IV

I now had a pure white room, with a white alcove, a white lady, black beams, and a red brick floor. What should I do with it? To be simple without being 'artily' simple, to be 'cottagey' without being self-conscious, to introduce comfort without marring the ancient pattern — this was the problem I had to face. And like all problems, it was solved in an unexpected way. It was solved by the red brick.

When the linoleum was first torn up, and when one had recovered from the horror of seeing loathsome insects, whose very existence was an affront to God, squirming about between the cracks . . . when all was clean and calm, I sat down on my packing-case, and rejoiced in the red brick. 'It shall be red brick, and nothing but red brick,' I proclaimed, in my innocence. And when they suggested that it would be cold, I said 'a fig for the cold' or words to that effect. And when they also suggested that it would be noisy, I made the same reply . . . for I love the sound of footsteps on old brick, footsteps echoing outside closed doors, the footsteps of servants going their errands, of friends moving about the house — even the ghost of footsteps, heard in the mind only.

But 'they' were right. The red brick was cold. And noisy. After a few days of it, I had a chill and a headache. Apart from that, it seemed quite impossible to keep it clean. You washed it, and though it would glow like rubies for an hour or so, by lunch time it was dim and drab. You brushed it, and it produced an inordinate quantity of dust from between the cracks. Also — worst trait of all — it developed a distinctly 'olde-worlde' appearance. Yes, even in the long-drawn twilights of summer, when the dying sun was like a golden stream retreating, the old brick struck a jarring note. Perhaps it was a supersensitivity that created this illusion

. . . perhaps it was only a vulgarized taste. But I shuddered to think how nearly the old brick resembled the linoleum that had vanished, how nearly it should have been spelt OLDE BRICKE.

From such shudders, such doubts, such fleeting ecstasies, was born the coco-nut matting. I do not know how, or when, or why, or where. I only know that one day, at some minute that was not particularly sparkling on the jewelled clock of Time, I said 'There shall be coco-nut matting.' And there was coco-nut matting. And it was good.

§ v

Now, this is fun. At least, to me it is fun. I did not realize, until I began to write about it, how the Garden Room had been built up . . . how it had evolved, slowly, like a puzzle, piece by piece.

First the white, then the alcove, then the coco-nut matting, that had the colour of unpolished wood, and felt charmingly rough underfoot, with a border of red brick at the sides.

And then, the blue Bristol glass.

There were four of these glasses. I had bought them for a shilling each, years before, in an old shop at Bristol, and I have felt guilty about them ever since, because I do not like striking that sort of bargain. However, if I had not bought them, somebody else would have come along. And anyway they were very lovely.

I took them into the empty Garden Room one evening at twilight, with the idea of filling them with flowers. By accident I set one of them against the window. And having done so, I sat down suddenly on the packing-case, with a thump, and forgot all about the flowers, and stared and stared at the blue glass.

This was perfect! Here, surely, was the ultimate blue! And yet . . . not the ultimate blue, for if one stared long enough, at this little glass set in the window, with the dying light about it, one saw a hundred whims and echoes of its own sweet nature. There was a blue that was caressed with green, where the shadows of the damson tree lay across it, and a blue that verged to black, at its edge, where the light faltered. There were spaces that seemed almost white, checked and spattered with dancing spirits, glistening with a filigree of silver leaves. There was a blue that was like the blue of secret pools, where the sigh of the sea comes softly from over the rocks, and the sky looks down in wonder at its own beauty.

All these blues were blended in my piece of Bristol glass. The light faded . . . the stars began to come out . . . the silver signs of the nightly carnival of heaven . . . the birds grew weary, threw their last plaintive notes across the meadows, rolled up their song-books under their quivering wings, and shut their eyes. A door opened, and from an immense distance I heard a voice saying something about dinner. But the smell of the flesh-pots drifted only faintly to me. There was still a little blue left in the glass . . . a deep deep blue . . . the blue of fathomless lakes, in which one star shone, like a lovely diamond. At last even this blue was quenched . . .

And I suddenly realized that I was very hungry.

§ VI

This is becoming more and more like the House that Jack built. Still, we must reiterate. First the white, then the alcove, then the coco-nut matting, with its fringe of red brick, and then . . . the blue Bristol glass.

And from that blue, everything else in the room radiates. It sounds frightful, and more arty than words can describe, but it was like that, and I believe that it is the best way to do things. For once the blue glass was set in the window, to my endless delight, the rest followed quickly.

For weeks I went about London clutching the blue Bristol glass, wrapped up in a piece of brown paper, and many was the delightful hour I spent unwrapping it in china shops, and furniture shops, to compare it with plates and fabrics. 'Compare,' is not really quite the right word, for I used to ask the glass questions.

'Do you like these curtains, O blue Bristol glass?' I would say.

And always I received an immediate answer. You would be surprised at the number of curtains it did not like. It took me a whole week to find a stuff with which the glass said it could be happy . . . but it was worth the trouble. For the material chosen was one of the most charming cretonnes you have ever known — a very simple design of blue cornflowers stamped on a pure white ground.

Sometimes, it seemed, the Bristol glass decided that it did not want blue things at all. It sternly vetoed any suggestion of blue in the chintz, for example, choosing a pale grey, with a misty design of yellow birds. It also chose, without hesitation, a pair of large, white, glistening china cocks, with yellow beaks, and observed, as it chose them, that it would like them put very close to it, on the old French Provençal table.

But usually, it demanded some echo of its own colour, and as I always obeyed, the room is full of blue echoes, that drift from chord to lovely chord as the pale fingers of the light caress them . . . the golden fingers of the day and the silver fingers of the night. There is a blue sky, for example, in a delicious little Early Victorian plate I bought in the Caledonian Market, which is painted with the picture of a young man felling a tree with a tiny hatchet and a ferocious expression. Underneath this picture is printed, in blue letters, the admirable observation:

> *Light strokes fell great oaks.*
> *Industry pays debts but despair increases them.*

The blue Bristol glass gave its instant approval to these highly moral sentiments.

There are also many blue echoes on my egg. I must explain my egg. It was originally a large, smooth, oval stone which I found in a field, one September morning, and bore home rejoicing, because it seemed exactly what I wanted to prop open the door of the Garden Room. But when I put the stone down by the door the blue Bristol glass for some unaccountable reason said 'I don't like that stone.' I could not think why, because it was quite a nice stone, of the ordinary brownish colour which stones usually affect. Still, the blue Bristol glass did not like it, so the stone was removed to the toolshed. And that, I thought, was the end of the matter.

But it was not the end. For the door creaked, and swung backwards and forwards, and had to be propped open with chairs which made abominable scrapy noises on the brick. I hankered after my stone. I used to go out and look at it, and wish I could have it back.

Then one day, I had a brain wave. I went into Peterborough and bought some white paint and some blue paint. Then I came back and made the stone white all over. When it had dried I painted large blue spots on it. The result was enchanting. . . .

For I discovered that, by a happy chance, I had laid an egg.

I have always wanted to lay an egg. It seems, really, the one activity against which nobody could possibly protest. To go out into a field, to peck a piece of grass which nobody wants, and then retire, to meditate, and suddenly to go pop, and wander off, with complete unconcern, leaving a beautiful clean egg on the grass . . . you must admit that there is nothing to be said against this behaviour.

Well, at last I had done this thing. And I took my egg into the house, and laid it before the blue Bristol glass, and the blue Bristol glass said 'You have laid a very nice egg indeed. You can put it on the floor to prop open the door.'

And everybody who comes in to the Garden Room, and sees my egg, says, 'But it looks exactly like an *egg*!' which makes me laugh.

I could write a great deal more about the Garden Room, but there are so many other things to tell you about that I suppose I had better stop. I do hope you have some idea how it looks? How the blues drift in and out, a note here, a note there? And how the Bristol glass presides over everything, giving the whole room its blessing?

If ever anybody were to break my blue Bristol glass . . . but I daren't think of that. This has been such a happy chapter. Let it remain so. For tragedy looms ahead.

CHAPTER IV

ENTER MRS. WRENCH

TRAGEDY entered with Mrs. Wrench.

A few readers may remember that in my previous chronicle of Allways I mentioned that when I first arrived the cottage was inhabited by a domestic devil named Arthur. After Arthur's dismissal, there was a record of the blessed relief occasioned by the arrival of my present housekeeper and her husband, who are both, happily still with me.

The long interregnum of Mrs. Wrench was not even mentioned. Partly because the matter was still extremely painful to the writer, but principally because she played no part in the story.

It is now very necessary to refer to this lady, because it was she who was a very potent influence in the cottage during these early days.

Mrs. Wrench was a Scottish widow, and needless to say, she came with the best possible references. Each employer for whom she had ever worked spoke of her in such ecstatic terms that it seemed difficult to understand how they had ever allowed her to be torn away from them. She was as honest as the day, as clean as a nut, as capable as Mussolini, and her cooking was a dream. So loud were the praises of the sheaf of letters which she sent me, and so varied were her accomplishments, that if a letter had arrived stating that Mrs. Wrench was, in addition, a trapeze artist, and a Dame of the British Empire, I should not have been at all surprised.

Needless to say, her arrival was awaited with impatience, tinged with trepidation. Those letters had made me nervous. They had not said anything about Mrs. Wrench's conversational abilities, but I was so worked up by these advance notices that I was quite prepared for the advent of some highly curved widow, smartly dressed, spitting *mots*, and tralaling French songs as she condescended to make an omelette. I saw myself miserably following her about the house, picking up her lipstick as she flicked an incomparably efficient duster over my humble bed.

It was therefore with considerable relief that I saw, stepping out of the village Ford a large, homely-looking woman of about fifty-five, with straight red hair, and very long limbs, dressed in simple country clothes. Her features were somewhat gaunt and forbidding, but that seemed as it should be. She was obviously extremely strong, because she used only one hand to carry a suitcase which had made the chauffeur stagger under its weight. A fleeting recurrence of the fear that she might, after all, be a trapeze artist, assailed me as I hurried to greet her. But these fears were soon put at rest.

Mrs. Wrench, apparently, was extremely normal. She looked at the stove and said she could 'manage' it. She examined the lamps. She could 'manage' them, too. As we went over the cottage, and examined each detail, she said she could 'manage' it. She also said that she could 'manage' coffee after dinner. As I left her, I felt that at any moment she would say that she could 'manage' *me*. Which filled me with gloom, because I am pliable and weak, and my back was specially designed for the accommodation, in large quantities, of old men and women of the sea.

But, no. Mrs. Wrench did not want to 'manage' me. She constantly asserted that she would soon 'get into my ways.' She also asserted that 'nobody could say she didn't try.'

Therefore, though I felt that I could never cherish any very tender emotions about Mrs. Wrench, she would do well enough.

§ I I

It would be difficult to say how the first signs of hostility manifested themselves. The causes of these domestic battles, like the causes of great wars, are obscure and far to seek. Master and man, mistress and maid — they begin as allies, for a time they work peaceably together, side by side, and then, gradually, there are frontier incidents, skirmishes, and at last, pitched battles, in which the maid, more often than not, is left in undisputed possession of the field.

Everything, it seemed, was going along very nicely. The odd man from the village (also a Scot) reigned calmly, if somewhat autocratically, over the garden. Mrs. Wrench reigned in a similar manner over the house. She was clean, honest, and a fair cook, although her Yorkshire pudding always had to be buried in the garden. She also said, with an irony which was not at first apparent, that she *liked hard work*. And as I was seldom at the cottage for more than a week-end, and then usually alone, I did not detect any undercurrent of double meaning in this phrase.

However, there was a very deadly undercurrent.

Here the reader must be convinced, if he is to bear with me in sympathy, that Mrs. Wrench's duties were by no means superhuman, and could, indeed, only by a vivid stretch of the imagination be described as onerous. For in those early days I was not able to spend nearly so much time at the cottage as I do now, and during most of that time I was alone. Besides, as we have seen, the cottage was nearly empty. Its accommodation, with the exception of the servants' quarters, consisted only in three small bedrooms (two of which were seldom used) two small sitting-rooms and one tiny hall. That was absolutely all, apart from what is euphemistically termed 'the usual offices.' These 'offices' indeed, were far from 'usual.' In fact they were so unusual that many people, when being taken over the house, gaily exclaimed, before I could hurry them past the door, 'Now *this* is the room I want for my sitting-room!' And then the sudden vision of an impolite object in a dark corner made them change the subject very hastily indeed, and remark that there was nothing like old oak, was there? To which I always replied that no, there really was nothing like it. After which, with mutual distrust, we would resume our tour of the house.

Of these five little rooms which Mrs. Wrench had to look after, four were, at the time of her domination, furnished so simply that they could hardly be described as 'furnished' at all. The Garden Room, it is true, was gradually taking shape, but my study held little more than a table, a chair, and a piano, while the bedrooms contained only a steel bed, a cupboard, a rug, and a washstand, on which reposed a pitcher filled with amber-coloured rain-water. They could all be 'done out,' by an energetic housemaid, in the course of an hour.

Therefore, the idea that Mrs. Wrench could possibly be overworked never for one moment presented itself. And it was not till after a long series of incidents, small in themselves, but all pointing in the same direction, that I realized what was the matter.

It began with a curious phrase which constantly came to Mrs. Wrench's lips. This phrase was, 'I was having five minutes.' She would say, for example, that the vicar had called during the week. 'I was having five minutes, after dinner, so he took me by surprise.' Or perhaps there had been a telegram which she had not known whether to open or not. 'But I was having five minutes when it came,' she would say, 'so I was able to deal with it all right.'

At first this singular phrase went in at one ear and came out at the other. It meant nothing at all to me. It did not suggest, as it ought to have suggested, the first rumblings of approaching thunder. No — it was merely an odd note, like some constantly recurring refrain in a long poem. Like, for example, the extraordinary couplet which echoes through the work of Blake:

> *The caterpillar on the leaf*
> *Repeats to me my mother's grief.*

A wild couplet, that, to which, in all solemnity, we may apply the tragic adjective *insane*. Such was Mrs. Wrench's constant assertion: 'I was having five minutes.'

A very minor incident gave to this phrase, for the first time, its full significance. . . I arrived, with a friend, an hour earlier than usual at the cottage.

I was feeling very happy that afternoon. The country was a paradise. The fields were dancing with buttercups, the hedges aflame with the sweet white fires of may. Over the wall the lilac leant its tipsy plumes, giving itself in lazy wantonness to the breeze. Every thrush was a nightingale, that day, and every starling a lark. And many were the thrushes and starlings and sparrows who fluttered into the air as I opened the gate of the secret garden, took a deep breath, and said, 'I am home.'

And then, framed in the window, a black figure appeared. Mrs. Wrench. Black not only in vesture but in countenance — a countenance made all the blacker by flaming red hair above it. She advanced heavily.

'You're early,' she said.

'Why yes . . . .'

Was it imagination, or did a cloud pass over the sun?

'*I was having five minutes,*' said Mrs. Wrench.
She stared at me reproachfully. I stared back.
She turned and went.

§III

I sat down on a tree stump. The phrase echoed
through my mind. My friend, whom we will call John,
was still fiddling with the car outside, so I was undisturbed.

Five minutes. Where had I heard that phrase before?
Anyway, five minutes *what*? It could not be prayer or
meditation, because Mrs. Wrench, as she often observed,
with her raven croak, had no use for the church or the
clergy. 'I know too much about 'em,' she would say,
as though she had spent years of research on ecclesi-
astical abuses.

Five minutes *what*? Was she, perhaps, engaged in
some illicit enterprise? Coining? Or even worse, taking
in other people's washing? Was she drinking? But no —
she was a teetotaler.

I could no longer ignore the obvious. Mrs. Wrench
meant that she was having five minutes respite from the
toils of slaving for *me*.

And yet . . . it seemed impossible. I had not been at
the cottage, during the last six weeks, for more than
three nights. Last week-end I was up for Sunday night
only. It was now Saturday. She could *not* mean what
she seemed to mean. Impatiently I jumped to my feet.
She must be sought out, and this dreadful problem must
be solved.

She was in the kitchen, washing a salad. As I opened

the door, I suddenly remembered that I had no particular cause to see her. So I said, on the spur of the moment, 'Oh, Mrs. Wrench, *have* you seen the bluebells in the orchard? They're too lovely.'

Mrs. Wrench inclined her head. 'Yes,' she said, 'I took five minutes off to go and have a look at them.'

That phrase again! I was as one hypnotized.

'Yes,' she went on, monotonously, 'I left everything, and went out, and I must say they're beautiful. Of course, I haven't seen them for a day or two, what with one thing and another, but I felt I just *had* to go and look at them.' She paused. And then, with the face of gloom which she always reserved for the delivery of an aphorism, she added, 'All work and no play makes Jack a dull boy. That's what I always say.'

§ I V

So it was true! I had been blind not to notice it before. And as I walked round the garden a whole flock of little memories pursued me, all revealing themselves, for the first time, in their full significance.

One of these phrases was 'it gives me a chance.' Every Monday morning, when leaving I would say good-bye to Mrs. Wrench and tell her that I would be up again on Saturday, to which the invariable reply was, 'Oh, yes . . . that'll give me a chance.'

Idly, in the car, I had often wondered what she meant. A chance to do *what*? To go away? Or entertain? Or stay in bed? No longer did I toy with these illusions. It was glaringly obvious that Mrs. Wrench meant that she would be given a chance to clean out my bedroom.

Again there was the phrase, 'I've got round.' Constantly, this was the first remark she made to me. 'I've just got round!' she would say — and I, poor innocent, concluded vaguely that she had been out for a walk, or had been in the kitchen garden when she heard the car. But no, she meant that during the week she had just been able to make the exhausting tour of my bedroom.

Now, a woman would, presumably, have seen these things long before, would have detected the delicate echoes of discontent, and opened immediate hostilities. However, my sex being of the gentler variety, I did not wish for hostilities. I wanted everything to go on quietly and peacefully. I wanted 'a good time to be had by all.'

There seemed to be no real reason for battle. It was surely only a matter for a little tact . . . a little adjustment? For, in all truth, Mrs. Wrench's position was *not* one of slavery. She was, to begin with, as strong as a horse. She ate enormously. She slept perfectly. For at least four days of the week she could stay in bed, if she so desired. I thought of the countless wretched general servants, in grimy London homes, who descend from their attics at six in the morning, who sweep, and brush, and cook, and run their breathless, soul-destroying race against time, day after day, year after year. If the 'family' are ever out to a meal, in such households, it is a red-letter day for these poor damned souls. God forbid that I should ever subscribe, directly or indirectly, to the perpetuation of such slavery. I would rather make my own bed, and sweep my own floor, and boil an egg over an oil stove than be served by the toil of such creatures. But surely, Mrs. Wrench's position could hardly be compared with theirs?

I decided to go and ask John what he thought about it. I found him in his bedroom, surrounded by piles of silk shirts, bottles, and tissue paper.

'I'm unpacking my own bag,' said John, rather loftily. 'I always do.'

I took a deep breath and was about to reply to this outrageous lie, when I checked myself. For I recalled that John was a Socialist, with exactly five thousand a year. He thinks that nobody ought to have more than exactly five thousand a year. (His last aunt died six months ago, and he has nobody else to leave him any money, poor boy.)

'Besides,' added John, taking out a large *flacon* of lemon verbena bath essence, 'one can never find things if one doesn't put them away oneself. Where shall I put this?'

I looked at it greedily. 'We might pour a little in the pond. The gold fish would probably grow horns.'

John, making no reply to this suggestion, put the bottle on the chest of drawers. There was already a formidable array of these bottles. They all had gold tops and little labels on which one read, 'The Hon. John ——, Hair Lotion Number 47A,' etc. Why John wanted these things, nobody can imagine, for nothing could be thicker nor yellower than his hair. However, I understood the purpose of the bottle of 'Iced Orange Water,' for use 'after shaving.' John does not like shaving at all. He shaves, indeed, with extreme petulance, because he hates to be reminded that he is growing up. The 'Iced Orange Water' was therefore, presumably, a consolation for this odious task.

The 'Iced Orange Water' being safely disposed of, John sat down on the bed.

'I think I shall leave the rest of the things till after tea,' he said. 'I can't imagine why Forsythe always wants to deluge everything in tissue paper.'

Which made me realize that although John might unpack, he certainly didn't pack.

The mention of Forsythe gave me an excuse for introducing the subject of Mrs. Wrench.

'Forsythe does everything for you, doesn't he?'

'What do you mean "everything"? He has practically nothing to do.'

'No — well — however — anyway he does everything. And he doesn't complain?'

'*Complain?* But my dear fellow, we're *friends*. Real friends. That's the secret of it. When I went over to Paris last week-end, I allowed him to lunch at the same table as I did on the boat. At the same table. He. . . .'

'Yes . . . you told me that before, several times. What I wanted to say was that Mrs. Wrench is complaining.'

'What about?'

'The work. She thinks there's too much to do.'

'There probably is a great deal.'

'But my dear John, I'm hardly ever here.'

'No — but when you are, there's a great deal. Besides it isn't only the work. It's the way you treat people. Now Forsythe . . . I always take him into my confidence. He's a friend.'

'And he lunched at the same table on the boat when you went to Paris, I know.'

'There's no need to be silly.'

'Well, how am I to take Mrs. Wrench into my confidence? What can I talk to her about?'

'She's a woman,' said John loftily. 'She isn't a machine.'

'I wish she *were* a machine. Machines don't look at you with a frightful expression as soon as you press the button.'

'Supposing *I* talk to Mrs. Wrench . . .'

'For heaven's sake, no!'

This almost broke up the conversation. However, peace was restored by my agreeing to John's suggestion that we should do our utmost, during the week-end, to make Mrs. Wrench's job as easy as possible. John confidently prophesied that after we had carried out certain little plans which he outlined, the whole atmosphere would be completely changed.

However, I had my doubts.

§ v

It would be tedious to narrate our many efforts to relieve Mrs. Wrench. How we carried out the tea-things, manfully declined to have coffee after dinner, fetched wood for the fire. As I said good-night to her, I looked for some sign of the change which John had so confidently prophesied. However, she only seemed to look a little blacker than usual. I sighed and decided that it was probably too early to judge.

The preparations we made, before finally retiring for the night, were exhaustive. We carefully scooped out the ash-trays, tiptoed with them up to the bathroom, washed and dried them, and tiptoed downstairs again, to place them on their appointed tables, retreating a few steps to see how clean and sparkling they looked.

We shook out the cushions and dug our fingers into the chintz seats of the sofa to smooth out the creases. We both made a vow not to sit on the sofa again in case we should disturb its marble serenity. We put every chair in its appointed place, and I swept the mud off the staircase carpet, using John's clothes-brush for the purpose. We polished the tumblers from which we had drunk our whiskies and sodas, and carefully deposited a saucer under the syphon, whose nose was dribbling. We poured water on the fire to put it out — a rather unfortunate manœuvre this, because it deluged the room with ash, which all had to be swept up again. Finally, we drew back the curtains, in order that Mrs. Wrench might come down in the morning to a room of sunshine.

The moonlight flooded into a room as clean as a Dutch interior.

'We can't possibly do any more,' whispered John.

'Unless we go up and undress Mrs. Wrench.'

'I'm quite tired, aren't you?'

'Exhausted.'

'I think I'll have a final whisky.'

'You can't. It'll spoil the tumbler.'

'I'll wash it out again,' said John, somewhat shortly. He then retired to bed.

In the morning I was the first to rise. We had decided overnight that we would make our own beds and clean out our own things on the washstand. I did this with a certain reluctance because, as we were returning to London that same night, I really could not see how Mrs. Wrench would occupy her time during the forthcoming week. However John had so impressed upon me the

71

necessity of treating her as a 'comrade' that I felt I really ought to be making Mrs. Wrench's bed as well.

I went along to see John. He looked so highly decorative in his pale blue pyjamas that it was a shame to wake him up. As I did so I observed that the room was still littered with the tissue paper from his suit-cases.

'You're going to make your own bed?' were the first words I said to him.

He yawned. 'What?' Then he blinked himself awake. 'Of course.'

'And you might empty things, too. I did.'

'All *right*.' He spoke somewhat gruffly, so I left him and went downstairs.

Mrs. Wrench was in the hall, putting two glasses of orange juice on the table. When she saw me her face fell.

'Oh!' she exclaimed, 'will it be earlier than usual?'

'It' meant a pot of coffee and four pieces of toast, which was all the breakfast we ever had.

'Oh, no, Mrs. Wrench.' I was bitterly disappointed that she had not made any reference to our beautiful clean room.

She breathed a sigh of relief. Then she pointed to the orange juice. 'I've got the orange juice done.' She spoke as though she had picked and pressed the entire contents of a large orange grove. 'I did it as soon as I got down. And then . . . Well, I mustn't waste any more time talking.' And she bustled out.

Somehow this conversation did not seem to augur very well for the future. However, the morning was too delightful to worry overmuch. There had been a ground-frost overnight, and the brilliant gold of the wallflowers was flanked with silver. It was one of those mornings when the air is so sweet and keen that you curse yourself for smoking, and throw away your cigarette on to the path, where it lies, sending up tiny mauve coils into the still air.

After about half an hour I returned to see how my Socialist friend was getting on. I knocked at the door.

'Come in.'

He was still not dressed. But the room was 'done.' That is to say, the bed looked as though a large body were concealed beneath the blankets, and little bits of sheet stuck out at odd corners. I made a mental note to come up and do it again after breakfast.

'Pretty quick work that, what?'

I agreed.

'There's nothing in it.'

'Inside the bed?'

'In doing one's own room, you ass. I wouldn't mind doing it every day of my life.'

'Then why don't you?'

'What?'

'And why do you say Mrs. Wrench has got too much to do if . . .'

A wild concatenation interrupted these inconvenient questions. John jumped.

'My God! . . . what's that?'

'Only the bell for breakfast.'

'*Must* she spring it on us like that?'

'It saves her coming upstairs.'

He gave me a sour look. 'Oh, yes. Of course.'

We went down. 'It' was reposing before the fire. I observed with interest that instead of four pieces of toast there were six. That must have been a great strain on Mrs. Wrench.

John rubbed his hands. 'You know,' he said. 'I could have done with a couple of eggs this morning.'

'I dare say that if you were to ask Mrs. Wrench she might make a superhuman effort, and boil one. But I think two would be a little much to ask, don't you?'

And I will say that John, although a Socialist, was decent enough to allow himself a reluctant grin. However, he did *not* go and ask for those eggs!

We will now leave Mrs. Wrench, for it is high time that we 'had five minutes' ourselves. But I warn you that we shall meet her again.

CHAPTER V

BY THE FIRESIDE

AND now let us stroll round and take stock of the situation, as it was at the end of those first six months. Let us link arms, and wander from room to room, bending our heads to avoid the low beams, which are not yet decorated with the warning floral signals. For unless we remember the blankness and the crudity of those early days, we shall not enjoy the days that are to come.

The first impression we shall get is one of coldness. You might almost say that the cottage looks *bleak*. For after the Montague horrors had departed, and all the cottage was whitewashed, summer set in, and the cool bare rooms, almost empty, very often dark, were exactly what I wanted. So I did not bother to fill them, or alter them. It was a very riotous summer, you may remember, when the sunlight slashed through the trees with the clash of swords, and the heat was arrogant, enveloping. A summer that took its toll of the flowers, breathing a scornful breath over the drooping roses, so that they gave up the struggle against this fierce lover, and hung their heads in weary ecstasy.

Yes — it was good to see the bare rooms in those days. If they were dark, it was a relief from the glare outside; if they were cool, so much the better. It never occurred to me that one day summer would end, and that when this happened, the darkness would be dreary, and the coolness merely damp.

Well summer *did* end. There came a day in late September when one realized that he had pitched his tents, blown out his fires, and set off South, carousing as he went, and hanging the trees with scarlet tokens, soon to be torn off, in anger, by the winds of autumn. And on that day I shivered, not only with cold but with apprehension, for I realized that I had done absolutely nothing to prepare for the winter.

It was this shiver which led to the first great engineering feat at Allways — the central heating.

§ 11

Central heating is still regarded, in England, as not quite 'nice.' If you say airily to most English country people that you have central heating, they colour slightly, and quickly change the subject, as though you had mentioned that you suffered from some complaint which was not normally mentioned in polite society.

Central heating, in fact, is still in the same moral position, in the year 1933, as hansom cabs in the year 1898. Hansom cabs, you may remember, used to be regarded as 'fast.' My grandmother used to say that any girl who sat in one must be a 'hussy.' What she would say about a girl who sat on a radiator, I cannot imagine.

Moreover, most English people still regard central heating as 'unhealthy.' They screw up their eyes and say 'oh, dear . . . doesn't it make the air very *dry*?' If you suggest that you prefer dry to damp, they say, 'but doesn't one catch cold when one goes outside?' Then they always add something about 'those dreadful hissing noises.' For you must remember that their recollection of central heating is mainly based on a night they spent in an hotel at Worthing, for Ada's wedding, in November, 1902. They occupied the royal suite, which contained the hotel's only radiator. This radiator, of Persian design, was the sort of thing over which savages would have built a temple. It hissed and gurgled and spat . . . it had mysterious cranks and pulleys . . . at noon it boiled . . . at night it froze solid. And housemaids approached it on tiptoe, with nervous giggles.

But always the main English argument against central heating is, 'Oh — but don't you like a *fire*? You're surely not going to give up fires *entirely*?' To which the answer, of course, is that you have not the faintest intention of giving up fires. Through the dark months of winter your rooms will dance perpetually in a maze of flickering shadows as the logs smoulder on the hearth. All you wish to point out is that if you have central heating as well as a fire, you will not be forced to crouch over a roaring fire, with burning cheeks, frozen ankles, your left leg scorched and your right leg numb . . . till you feel, at the end of the evening, like a badly cooked steak. No — you will be able to lie back, warm all over, and watch the gentle flames, and savour their beauty properly.

None of these moral or æsthetic problems worried Mrs. Wrench when I told her that I had arranged to go away for three weeks because the men were coming to put in the central heating. She was thinking only of one thing — the work.

'It'll make a pretty mess,' she observed.

'Yes,' I said, almost hysterical with cheerfulness. 'I expect the men will have an awful time clearing it up.'

77

This was not at all the remark which Mrs. Wrench had expected. She did not like to be reminded that the men would clear up their own mess. She wanted to project the painful mental image of herself wearily slaving through a tornado of dust and falling plaster. She moistened her lips and said scornfully:

'If they're like most men, they'll make more mess clearing up than they found in the beginning.'

Now, if the truth must be told, I had a sneaking suspicion that Mrs. Wrench might be right. For though the firm from whom I had ordered the plant had been most courteous — and though they had guaranteed to supply a boiler, pipes, and seven radiators, and do all the 'making good' for the very moderate sum of £75, I could not help feeling, as I looked at the staunch old beams and the solid bricks, that perhaps there *would* be a certain amount of 'mess.' However, it would not do to admit this to Mrs. Wrench. With a sort of wild vagueness I said:

'Ah . . . but these men are different.' I nodded mysteriously. 'Entirely different. You won't even know they're here!'

With which we parted, in a thunderous atmosphere. What that last sentence had meant I had not the faintest idea. It was a frightening sentence. It suggested a flock of peculiar fairies suddenly descending on the cottage, and floating round it with magical quietness. Men with tenuous limbs and enchanted fingers . . . men of whose existence Mrs. Wrench would not even be aware. It must have enraged Mrs. Wrench.

All the same, it was not so far from the truth. For the work was done with miraculous speed. And when I re-

78

turned, three weeks later, I stepped into a warm hall, spotlessly clean, with no stray pieces of plaster, no evidence of the turmoil that had been raging. And Mrs. Wrench could find nothing worse to say than, 'Well . . . we've got round!'

§ I I I

I swear that the cottage welcomed the central heating. Welcomed it personally, I mean.

For nearly four hundred winters it had shivered. With dismay it had seen patches of damp form on its old brick floors, shuddered at the mildew which had gathered, in sinister squares, on its patient beams. 'This will be the death of me,' the cottage had whispered, sadly, winter after winter. And only with the reluctant suns of spring did hope return to it, did the life blood stir and flow through its walls.

But now all was changed. In case you think I am making an absurd fuss about nothing, just consider what happens in the winter, when the afternoon is growing chilly.

I open the little door that leads from the hall into the kitchen. 'I think we'd better have the central heating on, don't you?'

'Yes, sir.'

I shut the door. Perhaps I go for a walk. Perhaps I wait inside. Anyway, in an hour or so, the pipes begin to get warm. I go upstairs . . . the water circulates first into the spare bedroom . . . put my hand on the little radiator . . . draw it off quickly . . . it is burning hot. In my own room it is only warm , , . downstairs it is just tepid. But all the time there is the sense of eager life flooding through the cottage, like the blood flowing back through the veins of a man who has almost died. There is a feeling of comfort creeping through the quiet rooms . . . of peace . . . of exquisite security from the cold legions of the winds, charging the gallant walls outside.

That is what central heating means to me. Lord, if we go on like this, we shall soon be writing poems to Frigidaires. Well — why not? To any man with poetry in his veins, the magic elixir flows through many strange channels. Of which, one of the strangest must surely be the little pipes that curl so cunningly round the walls of my cottage.

We will change the subject in a moment. But before we do, I must just mention that you cannot see these pipes. We have played charming games, concealing them. Sometimes they are white, sometimes black . . . sometimes a table conceals them, or a chair, or a piece of fabric, or a screen. Anyway, I defy you to come into any room in the cottage and see the pipes or the radiators without searching for them. You will only see white walls. But you will feel *warm*. Beautifully warm. And you will no longer feel that central heating is not 'nice.' It is very nice indeed.

§ I V

Where are we now? October? Well, let us say that it is October. The main thing to realize is that the cottage, with the exception of the Garden Room is still nearly empty, but that it is all white, and all beautifully warm.

It is like a lovely blank canvas, in perfect condition, on which we can paint as many designs as we choose. Let us gather by the fire, and all make suggestions about chintzes and corner-cupboards and lamp-shades and fascinating things like that.

However, I have forgotten a minor detail — which is that you still have no idea how large — or small — the cottage is. We will therefore make a very brief tour — the tiniest possible tour — partly because I don't think tours, in books, are very illuminating, but principally because I want to get back to the fireplace in my study. There is a story to tell about it.

We will therefore get the tour over very quickly.

You enter the cottage through a small lattice gate, step over about a yard of cobbles and knock at the front door, which is painted green and hung with a very pretty brass door-knocker that I bought in Venice, in a thunderstorm. You open the front door, and find yourself in a square hall, roofed with very thick beams. A tiny staircase runs up on the right, but we can ignore that for the moment. You walk straight through the hall, and find yourself in a tiny lobby — with the Garden Room ahead, another tiny staircase on the right, and the entrance to the study next it.

That is really all that happens on the ground floor, except the kitchen, which is round on the other side of the cottage. I do not seem to have told you much, but it is as much as you will get from most descriptions. And whichever way you turn you will see windows with flowers and vines peering through, and arches in the distance, and the shadows of branches on the ceilings, and a pattern of dancing leaves on the floor.

So shall we say that the Plan *has* been drawn, and the tour made, adding a hasty aside that there are three bedrooms upstairs, which will be explored in due course. And let us leave it at that, because I *must* get back to explain the fireplace in my study.

It is really a very inelegant fireplace. To be quite frank, it is not a fireplace at all, but a small kitchen-stove, dated about 1840, with a little oven on each side of it, and all those odd things which you pull out to make stoves 'draw,' and send sparks roaring up the chimney. (I never pull out one of those things without thinking that the whole house is going to be blown up.)

You would not call the stove actually ugly, because it is so small, and so very black and sparkling, and because one's eye is constantly drawn up to the minute ledge above it, which holds seven Staffordshire ladies drawing up their skirts in haughty contempt at the homely object beneath them. At the same time you could not call it pretty. It will not hold logs, and it is always sending out sudden fitful pouts of smoke. So why do I not get rid of it?

And here let us both be quite honest with each other. If I make a confession, you must meet me half way, and confess also. For the reason I do not get rid of my stove is the weakest, silliest, most indefensible reason in the world. Yet it is the most universal reason in the world, too, why men do not get rid of things. It is simply because . . . 'I HAVE GOT USED TO IT.'

When I first came to Allways, and began to show people round the cottage, I did not mind what they said about the stove, because I had every intention of getting rid of it. I did not mind at all when a slim girl with lips like wet poppies and hands that always seemed to be curved round the stem of a sherry-glass, leant against the wall and said . . . 'Darling, *how* frightful! We must pull it *right* out, and throw it into the very deepest ditch, don't you think? And make *endless* ingle-nooks, don't you think? And tell the *most* monstrous stories to each other on winter nights?' I really didn't mind, because it *was* frightful . . . and I had a sneaking feeling about ingle-nooks myself. I would like to sit in an ingle-nook all alone, and frown rather heavily, and ask myself what an 'ingle' was, and why it always lived in a nook, and if it had fun in its nook, and if it felt embarrassed, and slightly peculiar, when it left its nook. I would draw mental pictures of:

'An Ingle without its Nook.'

And very pleasing these pictures would be, when the nights were cold, and there was a hunger of unappeased love in a man's heart.

But gradually I began to get a little bored with the girls with lips like wet poppies. I did not respond so readily to their sneers at my stove. For things had begun to happen round the stove. Friends had told me stories round it . . . friends who were simpler and quieter than the wet poppy brigade. Chestnuts had been roasted on it. And in my head there was a pretty pattern of black and gold and red — the bars of the stove, the red of the fire, and the shadows on the faces of my friends. I wanted to keep those patterns . . . to keep them deep in my heart. Which was why I did not get rid of the stove. And why I never shall.

§ V

I seem suddenly to have stumbled upon a truth which
is both interesting and beautiful — like a man wandering through a wood, who trips over the root of a tree,
curses, turns back to see what has hurt him, and then,
if he is a sensible man, becomes absorbed in the sinewy
root which plunges through the dense earth, traces it
back to the trunk, and ends in a dream, gazing up to
the branches above.

This Getting Used To Things is one of the most important factors in civilization. For how else can we
explain why so many women put up with husbands who
are rotters, or why so many men put up with systems
which are rotten? Habit . . . the course which the river
of life has chosen for itself . . . that is the only thing
which prevents us all from going mad. Habit is also the
only thing which makes a house a home and not merely
a furnished apartment.

In a moment we will be leaving the fire and continu-
ing the tour of my little study. But since we shall be
meeting a great many bad habits during this tour —
vases that ought to have been destroyed and pictures
that should long ago have been banished to the tool-
shed — I do want to make one last plea for this
little weakness of habit. For we live in days when people
give orders to their decorators to 'do' a house, from top
to bottom, as though it were a purely impersonal
matter, and the result is so painfully correct that you
feel the women look out of place because they have not
got Chippendale legs. (Some of them have, poor dears.)

I can best defend Habit by reproducing a dialogue

once heard between a mother and her son about an old Victorian sofa. Admittedly, it was a brute of a sofa. It spoilt the whole room. The son had a real artistic sense, and he wanted his mother to get rid of it. This was what they said:—

Son: But mother — it's revolting.

Mother: Yes, darling. But you had measles on it.

Son: What has that got to do with it?

Mother: I don't quite know, darling. (Reflectively) Minnie had measles on it too.

Son (coldly): I suppose it was fumigated?

Mother: Constantly, darling. And that's another reason why I don't want to get rid of it. You see . . .

Son: I don't.

Mother: No, darling. You see, after Minnie had measles on it, the whole room had to be fumigated, and everything in it. And by some horrible mistake, one of the little kittens was shut up in the room — the grey kitten you used to call Cinderella, because she always wanted to sleep in the coal-box. The men came, and fumigated the room, and shut it up and sealed it . . . and we missed Cinderella. We called and called . . . and then I suddenly thought . . . and I ran out and got a ladder . . . (I remember stumbling over the step outside the tool shed, even now) . . . and I ran and put the ladder against the window and climbed up, and pushed aside the wistaria . . . (I can smell it to this day) . . . and I looked into the room and there was poor little Cinderella, lying dead on the floor. I couldn't believe it . . . I wanted to break the window in . . . but what was the use? She was dead . . . .

I climbed down the ladder, very slowly, thinking of

Cinderella, hoping it had been a quick death. I wondered what I should say to you. You ran out, just then, from the house . . . the sun shone on your hair . . . .

Son (impatiently): But mother, what has this got to do with it?

Mother: You were much fairer then . . . it wasn't till you were fourteen that you grew so dark . . . and you asked if I'd found Cinderella. I said 'No, I expect she's gone to see some relations' . . . and you asked me what relations she had, and I told you a little story about them . . . . it was a relief to tell you. You remembered Cinderella for a whole week . . . .

Son: And that was nearly twenty years ago.

Mother: Yes, darling. And that's why I'd rather not get rid of the sofa, if you don't mind very much.

§ V I

As usual, we have been led astray, and have lost the whole thread of the narrative. It is too late to pick it up now, or this chapter will never end.

And so let us pause for a moment, in my study. You remember the main facts? An almost empty room, an ugly stove, white walls? You also remember that we are *warm?* Well, there is one thing I have not told you about the study — a very sinister thing. It is still terribly *dark*.

With the conquering of that darkness, with the advent of a flood of light — (or to put it bluntly, with the creation of a window, among a great many other things) — we shall concern ourselves in the next chapter.

CHAPTER VI

OPENING OUR EYES

To me, all windows are magic casements. Whether they are bright or dim, whether they give onto green lawns or blink at barren bricks, or are shaded or sparkling, the life I see through them has a sweeter pattern. There is something terrifying about the wide spaces which the eye enfolds in the open air; and there are times in a man's life when he must always be darting his head from this side to that, watching from the corner of his eye to assure himself that the Enemy is not creeping towards him from the dim distance. But when he looks at life through a window he is safe.

Safe! And master of his own world. For with a tilt of the head, a cloud is banished, a green branch dances into view, the church steeple lifts its grey finger in the foreground, and the picture is perfect. A step to the side of the room, and the view through the window is utterly different, though no less delicious. For now the steeple is gone, and three poplars take its place; the hill gives way to a valley, the sky is a deeper blue, and across the foreground a swallow flutters, like a swift line in Indian ink from the pen of a Japanese artist.

Windows! Perhaps it is a weakness to wish, so often, to remain behind them — to draw the curtains, just a little, to frame the raggedness of life. And yet . . . I

am not sure. At least I know this . . . that it is better
to gaze through a small frame, clearly, than to walk the
open road with a downcast head.

§ I I

I had not been at Allways for more than a few months
before it gradually began to dawn upon me that the
cottage, in several places, was rather dark. And at first
this discovery was merely depressing. I did not realize
that anything could be done about it. You see, all my
life I had dwelt in houses which belonged to other people.
In my father's house, in rooms, in flats, and in poky little
places in Chelsea, where one had to sign dozens of
documents, and ask the landlord to dinner, and face to
the East, before one could even get the kitchen stove
repaired. Therefore, it seemed that if the cottage was
dark, one would just have to put up with it.

I don't quite know when I first realized that the
cottage was *mine*. I think it was on a morning in October.
You never saw such a morning — for the skies were as
blue as pimpernels, and the wind had a breath of smoke
in it, from some distant bonfire near a brightly-laden
orchard. It was one of those mornings which God
occasionally flings before a dull world as a great artist,
who is bored with his public, might fling his masterpiece,
crying 'Take it or leave it!' Never were there such blues,
such yellows, and never, never were there such reds, for
the maples, as I looked out of my window, were *en fête*.
They had been giving one of their last parties of the
year — you know the parties maples give. All night long,
in the keen frost, their faces had been flushed. Then

the rain had come, and they glistened in the yellow sunlight.

After seeing the maples from my bedroom window, the gloom of the study, when I came downstairs, was all the more marked. The sun had suddenly decided to sulk, and had retired behind a cloud of royal purple. And there was only a very inadequate pair of French windows in my study. I sat down to work. Half the paper was in darkness. It was hopeless. I should have to light the lamp.

Then, as I got up to find the matches, I paused. What was I doing? Why was I fumbling about for matches, when I could have a window, if I wanted? A window? A *window?* The inherited repressions of youth tried to close in on my brain, telling me that windows were impossible, that they were 'structural alterations' and that I should have to deliver Allways to my landlord in the same condition in which I had found it. 'But I am the landlord myself,' I cried! 'And if I like I can make the cottage one enormous window, at which I can sit and praise God!' Actually I said this out loud — so strange, so wildly exciting was this sudden revelation.

Yes, this was the first moment when I realized that I actually *owned* the cottage. That I could build out wings, and knock down walls, and paint it blue, and do all manner of things which I should not dream of doing. For a few ecstatic moments my mind was full of falling plaster . . . it rang with the hammers of masons yet unborn, it evolved ghostly staircases, projected strange gables. Only for a few moments. Because one cannot remain ecstatic for very long in so gloomy a light as my study afforded.

I stared at the dark wall. Slowly it seemed to open before me. The plaster paled, thinned, became transparent . . . there was a glimmering of branches, a stretch of lawn. Far away a fountain played, tossing tiny grey plumes against a tapestry of rich, mysterious oak . . . . A plague on these dreams. They ought not to come, like this, at ten o'clock in the morning. For there was only a dull wall in front of me, and I had entirely forgotten what lay outside.

Now if you are going to make a window, it is obvious that you must first acquaint yourself with the view which the window will give you.

I had entirely forgotten this view. I ran outside to look at it. And my heart sank.

§ I I I

Here, indeed, was a depressing outlook.

A dark, dripping corner of a wooden wall, with a very dreary laurustinus straggling up it, and a quantity of fly-bitten ivy. Even the path was melancholy, because the pretty red bricks stopped just before they reached this corner, and there was only mud and weeds. So much for my lawns and my fountains!

It would be terrible to look onto such a prospect, day after day, as one was working. Gloom and despair hovered only too evidently over this neglected corner. The very light itself would be tainted, as though it filtered through the bars of a prison cell. The only works that could be written in such a light would be morbid psychological novels in which monstrous little children sat under damp yews, discussing, in a Russian twilight, the suicidal tendencies of their parents.

There now began a delightful period in which we spent all our energies in brightening up this corner. I said nothing about the window, and the gardener thought it very strange that so much trouble should be taken about this dark and remote little corner of the garden. 'But no one will ever see it, sir,' he said, when I put forward various strange schemes. To which I only replied with a mysterious, and doubtless irritating, smile.

The first thing we did was to root up the laurustinus and the ivy. I hate rooting anything up, but this laurustinus was a thoroughly bad lot. There was no good word to be said for it, and when it was thrown onto the rubbish heap nobody had any regrets.

The disappearance of the laurustinus led to problem No. 1.

For having made this clearance there was now a wide gap between the little wooden wall and the lilac hedge. This sounds all right, because it meant that when the window was made, I could look out at the lane. But it also meant that when the window was made, the lane could look in at *me*. Which was quite another matter.

Now the traffic which passes down the lane outside my cottage is considerable.

In the early morning at least two carts trundle by, bearing sleepy ploughboys who sway up and down in their seats, regarding the dim horizon with cloudy eyes.

At about nine the lady from the post office arrives with the letters.

Between the hours of nine and six, several persons on

bicycles have frequently been observed darting by at a tremendous speed, with very angry expressions.

And in the evening, the traffic becomes positively delirious, because at least eight large boys assemble on the village green, and discuss world-affairs, with gestures as varied as their adjectives are monotonous. On stormy evenings, when there is electricity in the atmosphere, and the skies are like black curtains behind which strange spirits whisper, the blood goes to the heads of the village boys, so that they set out wildly for the Great North Road, a mile away. And there they stand, with flushed faces, hands in pockets, staring out at the cars which flash by, from one silly city to another.

Obviously, with such a whirl of life passing incessantly by my window, I should have no rest at all. The lady from the post office might see me, by mistake, and drop all her letters in confusion. The unknowns on bicycles might catch a glimpse of me, once a month, or even twice, and fall off their bicycles with the shock. The large boys from the village green would most assuredly see me, and the tension would be unbearable. You cannot possibly write 'I love you, Phyllis, God knows why . . . have I any chance?' when eight extremely well-developed boys, with their caps over their eyes, are glaring in at the window. You see, they know the answer to that question so very well.

Therefore, I had to block out this seething tide of humanity at all costs.

I blocked it out by extending the little wooden wall, and planting in front of it a winter honeysuckle, a berberis, and a cotoneaster. The honeysuckle comes out in February, and sends its fantastic sweetness drifting through the window, even when the snow is on the ground. The berberis is gay in spring and glossy-cool in summer. And the cotoneaster looks after the autumn months with the utmost charm and willingness.

On the other side of the wall I placed three laburnums. I planted them very small because I wanted to have the fun of waiting for them to peep over. They just managed it, for the first time, this year . . . and I shall never forget the thrill of that spring morning when, at last, two yellow laburnum blossoms, like tiny hands, fluttered over the top of the white wall. It was as though some child were outside, on tiptoe to look into the garden.

§ I V

And now the study was quiet at last, and white and warm and empty.

For a little while I let it be empty. I used to come down in pyjamas and a dressing-gown, on cold winter mornings, creep into the study, shut the door, and revel in the fact that the room was so warm, though there was no fire. I used to go to the window, and press my nose against the pane, and gloat over the snow that drifted up to the foot of the window, and rejoice in the icicles that hung from the water-trough under the eaves. There is something very exciting and beautiful about the shelter a little room like this can give you when the weather is grim and hard — when the wind rises and wails about the walls, in anger because it cannot get inside.

And then one day, the room was no longer empty. The front door was opened wide — gusts of snow and

frozen leaves scurried in (causing a look of fierce apprehension on the features of Mrs. Wrench, who was thinking of the work she would have with the carpets) —
the carters staggered in, very red in the face, the breath
steaming from their mouths, bearing a huge burden
covered in sackcloth. This burden they deposited in
the study. They unwrapped the sackcloth and there,
black and shining . . . was the piano.

I went out while they set the piano on its legs. I
always feel that a piano is a living thing and I hate to
see it with its legs wrenched off. I was still out when the
little piano-tuner came to give it a passage after its
trying journey. (He is a dear little piano-tuner, with
immense eyes, a weak chest and fingers like steel.)
It was quite dark when I came back . . . with the
song of the wind in my ears.

I opened the door. The lamp was burning by the
side of the piano, very low. I did not turn it up. I liked
to see the piano glistening there, in the half-light, very
black and shining. I went up to it . . . opened it.
The name of the maker — KAIM — shone out in dull
gold. I have never met another Kaim piano before, but
I swear it is as fine as any that was ever fashioned,
with a treble that is as sweet as clear water and a
singing bass.

I struck a chord, softly. The wind howled outside
and an angry handful of rain was flung by the distant
weather-gods at my lattice window. The lamp flickered.
I glanced at the window. So it was to be war, was it?
War between the music outside and the music in?
Very well, then; the challenge should be answered.
With trembling fingers I played the first tense bars

of Chopin's second scherzo — bars which are like some awful question, which is quickly answered by an arrogant flourish of chords. A tempest of rain beat against the window in the brief silence that comes after these chords. The lamp flickered wildly.

And thus, in tempest and in shadow, was the piano baptized.

§ v

Fifty years ago, when my mother was a little girl, she was asked by her governess what she thought were the saddest words in the English language. She pondered for a moment, and then she said, very softly, '*What might have been . . . .*'

'What did you say, child?'

My mother coloured. She gave her answer again. She tells me that she is not quite sure why she said those words. Sometimes, when I am sitting at the piano, I feel that I could tell her. For the only art in which I feel I could ever have been a master is the art of music.

Well it's too late now. You cannot do much by a few frenzied days with the Bach fugues, nor an odd week-end, here and there, puzzling over a full score, and wondering if you will ever be able to hear the wood-wind properly, merely by seeing it written. Still, it is agony to have to admit it. Agony to sit at the piano, on winter nights, with music rushing through your heart in a wild wind of melody, while you are only able to stammer with clumsy fingers, to fake chords, to muddle through a melody.

And so, apart from a few set pieces, and a few rare

95

moments when, somehow, my fingers seem to loosen, and acquire, by inspiration, a technique which is not theirs by right, all I can do in the service of music is to treat my piano properly. It is lucky that I made that confession before it is too late. For this book, as I have constantly to remind myself, is a book about a house, and nothing but a house.

So let us close the lid of the piano, reluctantly, and see how it is treated, in my study, as a piece of furniture. For it is much the most important piece of furniture in the room.

The first thing to observe is that it is *not* treated as a photograph gallery. For that is one of the habits of the English people which I have never been able to understand.

Have you yourself never thought how odd it is that in so many English households the piano is always chosen as the platform on which to place photographs of the ugliest and most hated relations? It is very peculiar. In exalted households, the piano is covered with pictures of Royalty. There is always a photograph of a woman with a hat like a frying-pan, signed, rather angrily, Louisa. There is also a photograph of King Edward, framed in silver with a little crown on the frame. Usually a field-marshal or two, in the background. And the customary assortment of Balkan princesses, clutching Pekinese dogs forlornly.

Why put these people on the piano? And why put Cousin Arthur, with the walrus moustaches, and Cousin Edwina, with three feathers perched on her head? When you are sitting down to play a Ravel saraband is it of vital importance that you should be reminded that Cousin Edwina was once presented at Court? And does it help you, in your struggle with Schumann's Carnival, to have Cousin Arthur's moustaches wobbling over you? If you ever try to play the Paganini Étude, in that enchanted musical procession, the moustaches will probably fall off. And then, where will you be?

But seriously, I think that most people are unkind to their pianos. They do not realize that they are magic caskets, which should be reverently approached — caskets which only a few privileged priests of music are entitled to open.

There is only one thing on my piano. (If I were a high-brow there would be nothing at all, but I am only a high-brow *manqué*.) The thing on my piano is a large white pitcher, splashed with green and yellow leaves. I bought it in Naples, years ago, and I put it on the piano one day, filled with apple-blossom, and played the twenty-third Chopin prelude to it. The sunlight danced over the keys, the apple-blossom swayed, ever so slightly, and because I had taken a glass of sherry, my fingers had no fear, and the prelude was perfect. You know that prelude? It is pure apple-blossom music . . . as delicate as fragrant, as the flutter of pale blossom against a blue sky.

§ VI

Round the piano are grouped a series of wool pictures. There is bathos for you, if you like. But it is intentional bathos. For when music means a great deal to you . . . when it speaks to you with a challenging voice . . . when the first bars of a César Franck prelude are like the tramp of a god over some distant hill . . . when the silver web of a Chopin étude is like a net in which you catch all the white butterflies of your dreams . . . then, you don't want striking pictures round you, or any bold pictorial design. You want everything to be subservient to the keyboard. That is why I like my wool pictures. They can mean anything, or nothing.

See that ship, for example. It was woven exactly one hundred and one years ago, for the number 1832 is very clearly discernible in a corner of the absurdly blue sea, which surrounds it. Well — it isn't really right, as a ship, but it is charmingly right as a picture to hang near a piano. The woollen wind is blowing the sails one way, and the flags another. The woollen clouds, with complete independence, are drifting yet another way. A few pieces of white wool indicate the angry surge of the waves, and a large woollen sea-gull hovers, with an expression of complete indifference, in the foreground.

This ship is a lovely thing to have over the piano. It is so primitive that your mind, inflamed by music, can make of it what you will. If it were a beautifully painted ship, with stays, sheets, top-gallants and all the rest of it, you would be distracted, would trip up in the rigging and be borne on unprofitable voyages. But my ship is so vague that it is really more ship-like than any accurate model could be. It is the soul of a ship — just as those early Ming horses, which are little more than a lump of china with four stalks stuck in the stomach, are the soul of a horse.

Abraham sacrificing Isaac, with the angel telling him

to stop, in a positive furore of yellow wool, is less primitive, and consequently a little more distracting. This picture hangs on the wall opposite the ship. I bought it, firstly because it is so beautifully woven (the oak-tree behind Abraham is worthy of the fingers of a Gainsborough), and secondly, because I was filled with a profound admiration for the moral qualities of the anonymous artist. To take so fiery and spiritual a subject, and then to decide to execute it in *wool* — this seemed to me to indicate a restraint, a stern, abiding purpose, which has sadly vanished from the world.

'How is Abraham's eye getting on, Emma?'

Can you not hear the gentle voice, echoing in the Victorian drawing-room, as the ladies bend over their work, before the lamps are lit?

'It is coming, mamma,' comes the dulcet reply.

'And the hand of the angel, Emma? Are you quite happy about the hand?'

'Not quite, mamma. But it will come.'

And the needles flash on, in the fading light.

I am not quite happy about the hand of the angel either, and I think that Emma, perhaps, got a little bored with it. Or maybe, Augustus came and sat by her side, and interposed a hand that was not so angelic but was, somehow, more exciting.

None the less, the picture has a strange, wild life, imprisoned in its gently-woven fabrics. It is the sort of picture, I feel, that might have been composed by one of the magic trio who sat in the parsonage at Haworth. The subject is discreet, the medium impeccable, the treatment conventional in the extreme. But there is a look in Abraham's eye that might have shone in the eye of Heathcliffe, and even though the wools are faded there is still a strange, unearthly radiance on the angel's wings, when the dying fingers of the evening sun are creeping down the wall.

§ VII

There are no books in my study. There are books in every other part of the house, but not in the study. When you are writing books it is embarrassing to be surrounded by the works of the masters.

'It has all been said before,' you mutter to yourself, as you look up, searching for a phrase.

'And much better said, too,' chortles the avenging imp who is always lingering behind the chair of any honest writer.

But though there are no books, there is a quantity of music, lying in a pile, on the red brick floor.

On the top of the pile is Bach's Italian Concerto — one of the greatest pieces of music ever written. I nearly wrote *the* greatest, although I realize the absurdity of talking like this about any work of art. There are a thousand 'greatest' melodies, just as there are a thousand 'greatest' poems and a thousand 'greatest' pictures, because there are a thousand moods in the mind of man when a certain note rings with the most clarity — when a certain design is most sharply silhouetted against the changing curtain of his mind. Aldous Huxley once wrote a delightful essay on the 'greatest picture in the world.' He was referring to Piero della Francesca's fresco of the Resurrection, which is so remarkably preserved in the Palazzo dei Conservatori at Borgo

San Sepolcro. 'The greatest picture in the world,' says Huxley. He adds: 'The expression is ludicrous, of course. But there does exist, none the less, an absolute standard of artistic merit. And it is a standard which is in the last resort a *moral* one.'

This is true. Particularly true about Bach. Here are the qualities of the Italian concerto. It is completely masculine. It is as virile a chant as ever echoes through the world. It is also completely *positive* — it sings the glory of God; there is no negation about it, no sad sighs, no doubting passages, for Bach wrote the first movement in the same mood that Shakespeare wrote that sonnet, whose opening lines are like a flare of trumpets:

Full many a glorious morning have I seen
Flatter the mountain tops with sovereign eye. . .

The Italian concerto is morning music: it flatters the mountain tops. Perhaps it is because one is so often in the valleys that one loves it, and drinks so eagerly from its eternal source.

'This is a book about a house,' whispers the avenging imp.

'Yes, I know. But this pile of music is a very important part of the furniture,' I reply.

'You ought to be talking about stair carpets and linen cupboards,' sneers the avenging imp.

Whereupon I sneer back, a little uneasily, and ask the imp if he has no soul? And before he has time to answer I am turning over the pile of music again.

Here are the Beethoven symphonies, arranged as duets. And often I have suffered bores gladly because they could read a good bass. I would not claim that I have ever got any tremendous emotional excitement out of playing these duets, because as soon as the main theme is announced one gets so excited that one forgets to count. Also it is agony when one comes to a little sort of five barred gate marked 18, which means that for eighteen whole bars the bore in the bass plays a solo. All the same, I have had happy times with those symphonies.

I must hurry through the pile because you are growing impatient. That big bound volume there is Brahms. That litter of very torn books contains the Mozart sonatas. The green leather case holds Debussy, Albéniz, and César Franck. Below are the Schubert impromptus, and the Schumann Carnival. There is a very precious little book of Couperin there.

Do you know Couperin's étude *The Waves?* It is tiny, so tiny that it could be played on a musical box; and simple, so simple that a child could manage it. Yet there is the whole grandeur and vastness of the ocean in it. That piece of music is, indeed, a perfect example of a storm in a tea cup.

There are a great many more excitements, for example, a Scarlatti invention so ingenious that the very line of the printed notes is pleasing, like some beautifully drawn geometrical problem. But, you ask me, what is that great heap over there? By itself? Well, that, I will confess, is Chopin. Yes, everything he ever wrote — the preludes, the waltzes, the mazurkas, the études, the scherzos, the rondos, the impromptus, all that glittering heritage he left us. I can't play any of them properly, but there is hardly a page which is not

stabbed with angry pencil marks, showing where I tried
to remind my thumb that it *must* hustle over a cadenza.

I am not ashamed of my love of Chopin. Very intense
young men sometimes come to the cottage, purr at the
sight of the Bach, smile patronizingly at the Beethoven
sonatas, breathe a sigh of ecstasy over my rather rare
edition of Stravinsky's second piano sonata, which is
completely unplayable and incomprehensible, fondle
affectionately the modern ballet music of Dukelsky,
but when they see the array of Chopin they push it
aside, and slightly curl their lips.

When they act like that they are given cooking-sherry,
before lunch. It has the strangest effect upon them, turning them rather white about the gills, and apparently
compelling them to tell me the stories of their lives,
which are always like the Stravinsky sonata — quite
unplayable and incomprehensible.

I abide by Chopin. He may not have known all there
was to know about life. Often, I feel, he battered his
white hands, feverishly, fretfully, against doors that
must always be closed to him; he tried to turn keys
that were too heavy for him; he sighed and wandered,
a prisoner, in rooms that were dark. But sometimes,
when the moon was high and the west wind was like a
dancer, drifting over the fields, he found the key — he
escaped from his prison, and danced beneath the moon.
And while he danced the night air echoed to the sound
of flutes, and the moonlit meadows were crazed with
melody. Even the white roses, on the wall, nodded their
heads so that you would think they were mimicking a
bar of music — a spray of buds here, pretending to be
a group of fairy crotchets; a full white bloom there,

like some exquisite semibreve. And thus the music and the moonlight and the roses danced into Chopin's heart, and went on dancing, dancing through his life, dancing through his death. For though he was a tragic spirit, he was really a gay one, too, and would not wish his melodies to be stilled merely because his eyes were closed.

And that is why we love him — we who are not afraid of being called sentimental. And that is why the pile of Chopin on my floor is so thick that Mrs. Wrench, when she observed it, always heaved a sigh and said how wonderful it was, the way things held the dust.

CHAPTER VII

EXIT MRS. WRENCH

Mrs. Wrench! I had almost forgotten her. She is so far away now — in years as well as miles — that I had quite a shock when her gloomy white face, with its halo of red hair, rose before me. Still, the very fact that it *did* rise before me shows how she darkened the whole horizon.

It was not that she did anything actually wrong. The cottage was clean, the cooking was fair. Moreover, she seemed to get on very well with the odd man. They used to talk Scotch together, in the spring twilight — she standing at the kitchen door (having five minutes, I suppose), and he leaning on his spade, with a nice cabbagy smell about him. He had a short grey beard which he used to pull from time to time.

The only minor complaint I could possibly have brought against Mrs. Wrench was in her voracious consumption of Vim. But then, that complaint applies to nearly all domestics. I am convinced that they eat Vim. Or else they roll in it, or sniff it up like cocaine or do something extremely peculiar with it, because no legitimate use of Vim could possibly account for the amount of it which is used in even the best-run households.

Apart from the customary consumption of Vim, Mrs. Wrench had all the virtues except the vital virtue of 'willingness.' You felt that her life was one long martyrdom of overwork. So strongly was she impressed by this idea herself, that you caught it, and worried for her.

The one benefit of all this was that she formed an inexhaustible topic of conversation. In those days I was moving about in a great many varieties of social circles, high, low, stupid, and intelligent, and I always found that if Mrs. Wrench were mentioned, she held the stage. The eyes of Cabinet Ministers lit up at the catalogue of her vices, and large, important women left conservatories, or wherever they happened to be putting spokes in the Wheel of State, and hung eagerly upon every detail.

'Of course, you should sack her *at once*,' they said in trembling voices.

'I suppose I should.'

'But *at once*. Too ridiculous — in these days. Why, there are thousands . . . thousands . . . she ought to consider herself an entremely lucky woman. How many bedrooms did you say?'

'Three.'

'And only two occupied . . . for week-ends?'

The large important women knew the answer to this, only too well, because we had it all out at dinner the night before. But they longed to be told it all again. They usually were.

Which made me think that Mrs. Wrench must be a universal figure. That she must loom, in the shape of a trusted lady's-maid, behind many toilet tables, that she must blacken many a domestic hearth, in nice middle-class families, and be extremely prevalent, as a dark 'daily,' in the houses of the poor.

However, in spite of her value as a topic of conversation, she was rapidly becoming so impossible that a crisis could not be far off.

§ 11

It began with a telegram.

I had arranged to go up to the cottage on Saturday as usual, with John. However, Friday morning dawned so exquisitely, so gaily, that even the roofs of Westminster looked as though they had been laid with gold-leaf overnight. 'It is a sin to stay in London on a day like this,' I said to myself, and I got on the telephone to John. Could he come up to-day instead of to-morrow? Yes — he would be delighted. I sighed with relief and arranged to call for him immediately after lunch.

When we arrived at the cottage, the little country gate that leads into the garage was closed. Normally, it was always open, so that one could drive straight in. But to-day, the strain of opening the gate would obviously have been too much for Mrs. Wrench, who had only had three hours in which to open it.

The next portent was when I walked along the path towards the kitchen, opened the kitchen door, and called out: 'Mrs. Wrench.'

There was no answer.

'Mrs. Wrench!' Still no answer.

Leaving John to look after himself, I went through to the front of the house. She was nowhere to be found. I ran up the stairs. And there she was, in my bedroom, surrounded by sheets, pillows, and blankets.

'Good afternoon, Mrs. Wrench.'

'Good afternoon, sir.'

She lifted a pillow as though it weighed a ton, and heavily put it on the bed.

'It's a lovely afternoon.'

She turned round and looked out of the window. 'Is it, sir?'

'But haven't you been out, Mrs. Wrench?'

'No, sir, I have not.' She looked at me as a tortured mulatto might look at a particularly sadistic slave-driver. 'I *was* going to take five minutes, and go up the lane, but then your telegram came. . . .'

Something began to boil in me. In a voice that cannot have been quite steady, I said:

'But why don't you take a whole day off, Mrs. Wrench, if you want to? Or two or three days?'

She continued to stare.

'I'd take from Tuesday to Friday, if I were you,' I went on, madly. 'And just go out, or stay in bed, whichever you prefer. I think that'd be a good idea.' With a frantic effort I smiled at her. 'We'll have dinner at seven-thirty, I think.'

I then went down, tense with rage, knocked my head against several beams, and poured out my troubles to John.

§ I I I

Now John, in the previous chapter, was a Socialist with only five thousand a year. But since then a great many things had happened. An obscure cousin, of whose existence he had previously been unaware, had been bitten by a snake in Bolivia, had expired, clutching John's photograph to his breast, and had left him *another* five thousand a year. And though one can be a Socialist with a mere five thousand (provided one spends enough time in the South of France, and has a valet with whom one can lunch in the Blue Train without any-body thinking it odd), it is a little more difficult to do it on ten.

So John had changed, and had become a Fascist. Fascism, in those days, was mercifully confined to Italy. The youth of England had not yet begun to prance about the streets in black shirts, like perverted Morris dancers, pushing the palms of their hands in the faces of a startled bourgeoisie, and selling them sheets of bloodthirsty gossip at twopence a time. No – the Black Shirt in the time of which we are writing, was still a distant menace. It flashed across the screens when Mussolini was in evidence, and housemaids giggled at the funny way in which the foreign troops stuck out their knees. But the idea of black shirts in England. . . .

However, John was always in the vanguard. Besides, a black shirt emphasized the pale gold of his hair. That was really the chief reason he became a Fascist, I believe, although he had certainly mastered the Fascist 'philo-sophy' very prettily. Especially in its application to women.

'Woman,' he said, bending down to pick a grape-hyacinth, which he carelessly pushed into his buttonhole, 'should be man's Helpmeet.'

John had a way of talking about Woman, in those days, as if she were a large marble animal, with no relations. He somehow managed to make the capital 'W' seem an essential part of her anatomy.

'I know,' I said irritably, 'but Mrs. Wrench isn't Woman. I mean she isn't a bit abstract, like that. She's got red hair and a turn-up nose. And really the idea of being a Helpmeet. . . .'

'I'll talk to her,' said John, tugging at the collar of his black shirt, and turning towards the house.

'Now, John . . . we can't go *entirely* without dinner.'

'Why should we?'

'Because she's got a grievance, and if you went butting in, she'd go.'

John snorted, pushed out his chest, and proceeded to pour scorn on me for my weakness. I, in turn, tried to point out to him, that Mrs. Wrench was *not* Woman, but a woman, and that she was not in the least like the sort of creature one sees on the wrapper of patriotic magazines, covered with corn-sheaves, and surrounded by Australia, Canada and South Africa (personified by bloated infants, playing about her feet). And that the word Helpmeet, to her, was not at all pleasing . . . it did *not* suggest stirring the pot for the returning warrior (while she suckled Australia, Canada and South Africa in the pantry) . . . but it *did* suggest making an extra bed and opening an extra tin of sardines.

'You're impossible,' said John. 'You go entirely the wrong way about it. Look at me and Forsythe. I've only got to lift my finger. . .'

'And he comes and lunches at the same table when you're going to Paris.'

John stared at me coldly, and resumed, 'to lift my finger, and he knows his place.'

'That sounds agony for both of you.'

'I beg your pardon?'

'Lifting your finger and knowing your place. Like a frightful parlour game. Somebody says, "Peekaboo," then you all have to rush out of the room and stand in a draughty corridor breathing in each others' faces, while some woman in pink giggles round the house with an old thimble. Really! What odd things you do with your servants!'

It would be unprofitable to continue this argument. After a time John calmed down, became a little less Fascist, and a little more human. Instead of making a raid on the kitchen, and delivering an oration on Womanhood, he agreed to wait till dinner-time and take part in a little scheme which I outlined to him, as we walked up and down, under the curdling, twilit skies of spring.

§ IV

By the time that dinner arrived I was in a state bordering on hysteria. Mrs. Wrench had informed us that we should have to dine off cold tongue — a depressing prospect in any case, rendered even more depressing by the acid remarks which had accompanied this information . . . such as 'the country isn't London, sir, you can't just run out round the corner.' Lord — if only Mrs. Wrench *would* just run out round the corner, whatever that meant, and never come back!

When Mrs. Wrench dumped the cold tongue in front of me, and lumbered to the sideboard to fetch the wine, I turned to John, and in trembling but crystalline tones observed:

'I think it so wonderful how your mother, with only one servant, manages to give all those marvellous dinners.'

John gulped. He had not been quite prepared for this. 'Er . . . yes,' was all he could manage.

'She bakes the bread too, doesn't she?'

'Who?'

'Your servant . . . Ada, isn't that her name?'

'Ada?' Another kick. Then he pulled himself together. Mrs. Wrench was now just behind me, pouring
out the wine, and I was able to give him a wink.

'Oh *Ada!*' He nodded gravely. 'Yes . . . of course,
she bakes deliciously.'

'And helps in the garden?'

'A great deal. And then, of course, the massage takes
up a good deal of time.'

'The massage?' This was a stroke of genius. I cast a
furtive look at Mrs. Wrench's face. It was as black as the
blackest thundercloud that ever loured over the Black
Mountains.

'From ten to eleven,' said John, warming to his task,
'my mother is always massaged by Ada. From eleven
to twelve she bakes. From twelve to one . . .'

A raven-like croak interrupted us. It was Mrs.
Wrench. She said:

'Will there be anything else, sir?'

'Anything else?' With hideous brightness I smiled at
Mrs. Wrench. 'Well, have you made anything, Mrs.
Wrench?'

I waited for the reply as one waits who has cast a
stone into a deep well. And after a pause, *de profundis*,
the reply came:

'No sir, I have *not*.'

The hideous brightness continued. 'In that case, we'll
just have coffee.'

She turned to go. She was half-way through the door
when I called out:

'And Mrs. Wrench — as it's such a lovely night, I think we'll have coffee in the garden.'

There was no reply. All I remember is that the black cloud in the doorway swelled, deepened, prepared to burst, thought better of it, and vanished. The echoes of the slamming door rang through the house.

'Well,' said John, 'that's done it.'

§ v

However, so weak is man, so subtle and clinging is woman, that by the time the morning came, I was full of regrets for my harsh treatment of Mrs. Wrench . . . anxious to make amends . . . eager to conciliate her. For I could not believe that she was wholly malevolent.

The whole problem was discussed with John, after breakfast. 'You should sack her,' he said.

'Listen!'

There was a muffled thud upstairs.

'That's Mrs. Wrench, making my bed.'

A quarter of an hour passes. The noises still continue.

'But what is she *doing*?'

There came the sound of heavy furniture being dragged across the room. Stamp, stamp, stamp; rattle, rattle, rattle. A pause.

'But seriously what *is* she doing?'

'Is it spring-cleaning?'

I shook my head. 'That was finished three weeks ago. Don't you remember? I went to Paris . . . "to give her a chance".'

'Perhaps she's burying something?'

Crash, bang!

'Perhaps. But she doesn't seem to have quite killed it yet . . .'

More draggings. The stampede continues, grows in fury. Suddenly there is a lull. We look at the clock. Since the first onslaught began Mrs. Wrench has been in my room nearly forty minutes.

'I think I shall go mad, don't you?'

'Raving. Couldn't we go and see what she's doing?'

'I wouldn't. Think what happens when you wake mediums up.'

'What happens?'

'They die. In an orgy of ectoplasm.'

'Do you think she's in a trance, then?'

'Well, can you think of any other explanation?'

'None. Oh hell . . . what *is* she doing?'

And thus and thus. Finally we gave it up. We went out. As we passed through the hall we met Mrs. Wrench coming down the stairs. She looked as if she had just cleaned out the Vatican, single-handed. Very timidly I said to her:

'Oh, Mrs. Wrench, do you think we might possibly have lunch at one, instead of half-past to-day?' (Lunch is some more cold tongue, some salad and some cheese. Mrs. Wrench never learned to cook an omelette.)

She passed her hand wearily over her forehead.

'I'll see what I can do.'

'Oh thank you, Mrs. Wrench.'

'But if it's *five* minutes past . . .'

'Oh that'll be quite all right . . .'

'After all,' she intoned, as a parting shot, 'I've only one pair of hands.'

She slammed the door. I paused and reflected that

114

this statement, after all, was true. Though anybody who listened to the noise upstairs would say that she had ten pairs of hands, and twenty pairs of very large feet.

I went upstairs to see if, by any chance, she had pulled down a few beams or torn up any boards. No. Everything was as it should be. The small bed stood in the corner. The one table and the one chair were in their appointed places. I could have turned everything in that room upside down, emptied a sack of soot on the floor and had it all cleaned up again in half an hour. Mrs. Wrench, with none of these disadvantages, took twice that time.

What did Mrs. Wrench *do*?

§ VI

The time has come when we must invoke that imaginary veil which the novelist so often draws out of his inkpot when the situation of his characters becomes too painful to record, or when, as I suspect, his inspiration begins to flag.

The veil, in this case, was provided by the arrival of a telegram which I received, not long afterwards, from the odd man. It read:

Mrs. Wrench left this morning shall I sleep in Parsons

My first feeling on opening this was one of the utmost relief. I thought of the cottage, relieved of that terrible brooding presence, and never had it seemed more precious to me. Now it really *is* mine! I thought, and almost made up my mind to have nobody in it at all, to let it get beautifully dusty, and to dine off endless tins of delicious sardines. But then, I began to wonder what had happened.

I learnt, as soon as I arrived at the cottage. Mrs. Wrench had come into a fortune! It was variously estimated at sums ranging between five thousand pounds and a quarter of a million. The people who hated her most, strangely enough, were those who were most positive that her fortune was immense.

This news was not quite such a shock to me as it might have been. I had often wondered if there was some mystery about Mrs. Wrench. For instance, from time to time she would receive bulky envelopes by registered post, and on more than one occasion she had asked me to witness her signature to a legal document. I never read the documents, and had not the remotest idea of their nature. It was now very evident that they had been transfers of stocks and shares.

It was only gradually that I was able to piece together the full story of her departure, and it is too long to give here. But the main facts are as follow:

On the morning when the odd man sent me the telegram Mrs. Wrench suddenly appeared in the kitchen door, dressed, as the old man described it, 'Like nobody.' She wore a fur coat, silk stockings, shoes with very high heels, and she carried a silver-mesh bag. In a hoarse and lofty voice, without a trace of a Scottish accent, she commanded the odd man to take her suit-case to the village Ford, which at that moment arrived outside the door. He was so thunderstruck that he obeyed, gazing at his late companion in awe. As they walked down the path Mrs. Wrench briefly informed him that she was leaving for good, as she had come into money, that she did not propose to give any address, as she was going to Canada, and was sick of the sight of England, and that she would 'waive' the question of any wages I might owe her. As she had been paid in advance, 'waive' seems the right word.

That was absolutely all. She was off, in the Ford, before any more could be said. And from that instant, a darkness as deep as the grave descends on Mrs. Wrench. There is one brief flash of light, at the station where, for a moment, the astonished porters saw her entering a first-class carriage. But after that . . . there is darkness. Let her rest in it.

A few days later, the S.s arrived, and from their arrival dates the Age of Peace. I no longer felt like an intruder in my own cottage. And I no longer had to wonder if it would be a terrible strain if anybody were asked in to have a glass of port after dinner.

The Kitchen

CHAPTER VIII

RAIN ON THE ROOF

Soon after the S.s arrived, the Great Drought began. Although it was only the beginning of May, the skies remained, day after day, like a sheet of blue enamel, without a single flaw. This Great Drought was the direct cause of many exciting developments at Allways which we shall narrate in due course. I think that some of these developments were due to the state of emotional tension which a drought always seems to induce.

It is terrible to walk through a garden in a drought — almost as terrible as walking down the Thames Embankment during a bad spell of unemployment. You want to water all the poor flowers . . . you want to give all the poor devils money. There are only a few buckets left in the water butt, and only a few shillings in your pocket. What are you to do?

It is at times like this that one wishes one were a cow, or some other nice ruminant animal, that didn't worry.

Therefore, we stay indoors, waiting for the rain.

Now in case you are getting impatient, I would remind you that there was once a great man called Pascal, who delivered himself of the wisest generalization about Mankind which has ever echoed through this dusty world. Do you remember it? Pascal said: '*All the misfortunes of man arise from one thing only, that they are unable*

to stay quietly in one room.' Well, you stay quietly here with
me, during that second June at the cottage, towards the
end of the Great Drought.

For really, the rain is coming, very soon, and when
it has come, and when a million scents of saved souls
are drifting through the window, we can get on with the
story. You won't care, by then, because the savour of
flowers and leaves after rain will have drugged you into
a merciful oblivion.

We are still waiting for the rain, in our quiet room.
The barometer, of course, is haughtily unaware of the
fact that the skies are clouding and that a tiny breeze is
blowing through the hedges.

If your barometer is in the least like mine, it may
be likened to a guest who arrives extremely late at a
party with news which we have all been discussing for
the last three hours. My barometer registers 'Very
Dry,' with unfailing fidelity, until the thunderstorm is
over. Like those tiresomely amiable women who say
'Such a success' about all marriages, even when the parties
concerned are bouncing about on the wrong sofas with
the wrong people under their very noses. And then,
when the hedges are dripping, and a muddy torrent
swirls down the garden stream, and one is in a fearful
state about the Canterbury bells, whose pale pink faces
are spattered with mud, the barometer very cautiously
and tremulously takes a step back. Just as the amiable
women, when it was all over, breathe a faint 'I told you
so.'

Barometers and politicians, one might say, at random,
have much in common. They are always wise after the
event. I feel that Mr. Asquith must have first said those

melodious words, 'Wait and See' — while he was tapping a barometer at The Wharf, to see if the rain outside was real rain, or just an illusion, like the German bombardment.

§ 11

At last the rain came. It came like a long-drawn sigh — a faint patter on the leaves, that at first I thought was the wind. And there was a ghostly, hesitant tapping on the roof of the tool-shed, as the big drops fell, one at a time. I liked the rain to come like that in big drops, sulkily, because it heightened the exquisite suspense of wondering whether these drops were only stray visitors, on their own, or whether they were the vanguard of a host that was following from above.

When the rain came in those big, solemn drops, there were a thousand excitements to be noted while I sat quietly by the open window, like a good little student of Pascal. For instance, the first drop of rain fell straight on to a volume of Keats's poems which had been left open on the little garden table outside. I hurried to fetch the poems, and as I put my hand out for the book, another drop fell, almost in the same place. These two drops had fallen, like tears lately shed, on to the loveliest lament Keats ever wrote —

> O Sorrow!
> Why dost borrow
> The natural hue of health, from vermeil lips?
> To give maiden blushes
> To the white rose bushes?
> Or is it thy dewy hand the daisy tips?

There, on the poem, the raindrops glittered, as though they were Keats's own tears. The rain fell, the print dimmed . . . the lovely words were dissolved in Sorrow's dew. It was as though a cloud had drifted over the open book and, growing heavy with sadness, had shed itself in the poet's memory.

§ I I I

Still I stayed indoors, drugged by the rain. The books had been taken in, and the cushions, and the deck-chair was folded under the eaves. The rain was coming down, fairly heavily. And I sat by the window, as though hypnotized, as though the rain were falling for me alone.

Any good gardener will know what I mean. For when the rain comes, after a drought, he is *himself* the thirsty soil . . . it is his own agony that is being relieved . . . his own soul which is being saved. In spirit he bares his breast and sighs with delight, as the trees sigh when the water trickles down their trunks . . . in spirit he closes his eyes, as the lids of the flowers are closed by the merciful rain . . . 'More, more!' he cries . . . and always there is the sense of life returning, as it returns to the fainting leaves.

And how busy and anxious and tiresome he is if the rain seems likely to stop!

'Will this have done good . . . is this enough . . . surely this *has* done some good?'

The gardener always says 'It ought to go on for another three hours before it'll do much good, sir.'

But in the sky there is a dreadful patch of bright blue appearing! And that lovely angry-looking cloud, that seemed about to come down in a great deluge, has turned out to be a sheep in wolf's clothing, for it is producing nasty little fleecy edges, and is starting to caper away, over the hills!

'Oh, come down . . . come down . . . go on . . . please don't stop!'

The amount of energy I put into these invocations was tremendous. It was, of course, as useless as the energy we expend by pressing the feet violently on an imaginary brake while being driven by a snorting sportsman on a slippery road. Still, it was a form of energy that I could not control. I felt that if I stopped looking out of the window for one moment the rain would cease.

'Surely this *must* have done some good . . . don't you think this will be enough?'

But I never waited for a reply because I knew that it was not nearly enough. The soil under the hedges was still dry and caked. It must grow dark before the rain can be said to have really soaked through. And indeed, if it weren't for the fact that I had been watching the rain against a dark background, it would hardly have been possible to tell that it was raining at all.

§ I V

But at last it really came down 'cats and dogs'. The anxiety was over. And the itch of exploration was upon me.

For now was the time to put on an old mackintosh, and fetch an umbrella, and trot off to see what had happened. The first place to visit, of course, was the

greenhouse. Here there was a glorious gurgle going on
in the tank, and all the panes were clear and glistening.
Then there was the pond. It was rising visibly, and the
goldfish looked happier than they had looked for weeks
. . . darting about . . . peppered with rain drops. Then
the stream at the bottom of the orchard . . . it had
swollen to a torrent . . . and chuckled and hiccuped and
tumbled, like the dirty little ragamuffin that it was. And
then there were all the flowers . . . but that would take
us far too long. Besides there was a sudden urgent
summons from the house . . . a bell ringing violently
. . . what was it?

Well, 'it' was the something which I have promised so
often in the past few pages . . . the resumption of the
story. We must therefore return to the narrative, summoned by that tinkling bell, which sounded one stormy
day in June, not many years past.

I ran back to the house, folding my umbrella.

'What is it? What is it?'

'It's the thatch, sir. Simply *pouring* through.'

'Oh Lord.'

'I always told you, sir, we ought to have it done.'

'I know. Have you put anything underneath?'

'All we could lay hands on.'

'All right. I'll go up and see.'

I ran upstairs. Into the blue bedroom. There in the
doorway, I paused.

It was indeed a dismal sight. Large patches of the
ceiling were grey. Through several cracks ominous
little streams were running, streams of water rendered
milky by the whitewash. Pieces of damp plaster were
scattered about the carpet. All that could be done to

meet the onslaught had been done. The little room echoed with the shrill trickle of water falling into basins.

Dismal . . . yes. Dismal . . . y-y-yes? Dismal . . . *no!* There was something gloriously exciting about this disaster. It was a challenge of the elements. All about me was the smell of old wood and clean linen. Outside the rain was shooting a million swift arrows of silver, again and again, into the quivering bosom of the earth, on to the proud leaves of the trees, against the frail roof of my cottage. At such a moment I and the cottage were one. We accepted the challenge, gladly. We declared war, together, on the rain . . . the rain that so lately had been our friend.

I ran downstairs and sought out my houseckeeper.

'To-morrow,' I cried, 'we shall send for Mr. Penthrift!' And even as I said it, there seemed to be a slight lull in the rain, as though it had heard, and taken fright.

For Mr. Penthrift was the best thatcher in the whole county of Huntingdon.

CHAPTER IX

REEDS IN THE WIND

MR. PENTHRIFT looked exactly like the Duke of Wellington. He was not so tall, it is true, and there was a twinkle in his eye which I have never associated with the Gentleman of Iron. But when I first saw him, standing outside the front door, on a summer evening, the resemblance was uncanny. The same chin, the same mouth, and most important of all, the same nose.

But the resemblance, happily, was only profilic. Mr. Penthrift could not have had a gentler, kindlier nature. He gave me the impression that he loved thatching so much that if he could have afforded it, he would have done my roof for nothing.

The price was the first thing we discussed.

'Well, it all depends on whether you have reeds or straw,' said Mr. Penthrift. 'And then again, whether you'll be wanting any diamonds.'

'Diamonds?' I looked at Mr. Penthrift sharply. Was he suggesting that the roof was to be encrusted with precious stones?

'That's what they call the little pattern we make, sir, on the ridge.'

'Oh, I see.' In some ways I was rather sorry to hear this. It would have been nice to toy with the idea of a cottage with jewels glistening from the roof . . . with bands of emeralds round the windows and the front door thick with rubies. On moonlight nights it would have looked like an immense toy, carelessly dropped by a giant in the quiet lane.

'Will it be reed or straw, sir?'

'Which do you think?'

'Well, of course, the reed'll last much longer. A good three hundred years, the reed'll last. But the straw . . .' and here Mr. Penthrift wrinkled his nose a little contemptuously . . . 'The straw'd have to be done over again after fifty years.'

A mere fifty years, in the life of my cottage, seems nothing at all. So the idea of thatching it with straw was obviously out of the question. Hardly would the straw be in place before it would have to come off again. It would be like putting on a hat to go to the pillar box at the end of the road.

So though Mr. Penthrift told me that the reed thatch would cost a hundred and sixty-five pounds, I decided to have it.

§ 11

I asked him where, and when, he found his reeds. He took a pull at his pipe and said:

'In Fallow Water, sir . . . that's where the fen ends, over Ramsey way. We fetch the reeds in December and January . . . that's the best time. They grow six foot high in the ponds round there. A flat-bottomed boat's the best to fetch 'em in. And you have to take 'em off below the water, with a sharp scythe. It needs a knack. . . .'

Since then I have been reeding, on winter mornings,

in Fallow Water, and I can bear out the truth of Mr. Penthrift's statement that it needs a 'knack'. When you first grip the scythe, and plunge in your arm, nothing happens. You only bruise the poor stems of the reeds. And even if you cut them, you only cut a few, which fall in the wrong direction, away from the boat. It needs skill and practice to bring them down in a proud sweep, with their plumes towards you.

This is what happens when I go reeding:

It is a dark, cheerless morning, with an icy wind coming over the fens. Though it is nearly nine o'clock the sky is still night-stained, and only a pool of watery yellow in the East shows where the sun is hiding. But I have had a good breakfast, and am wearing the thickest coat I could find so that I am not cold. Besides there is something so exciting about this little adventure that the blood runs more quickly through one's veins.

The little boat is waiting, half hidden behind the reeds. We enter it and push off.

'A cold morning,' says Mr. Penthrift. His nose is now bright blue, making him look more like the Duke of Wellington than ever.

'Very cold,' I reply. And that is all our conversation, for the work is beginning.

We paddle the little boat towards a cluster of reeds that rises, like some fantastic city, over the black water. A gust of wind blows up, and there is a sudden wild whispering among the leaves of the reeds and in their brown feathery crests, as though they knew that their day was ended, that they were about to fall, cut down cruelly by the enemy that is coming from under the water. Sometimes, when we have come to a particularly beautiful cluster, whose stems thrust themselves proudly, six foot above the surface, whose leaves are very green, whose plumes are very gallant, I have hesitated before cutting them. They seem so happy out here, in the lonely fen, with the secrets of the water about them, and the cry of the wild fowl.

However, one has no time for sentimental musings when Mr. Penthrift is about. The boat is brought to a standstill. You lean forward, grasping your curved scythe. You bare your arm, take a deep breath, and plunge it into the icy water. Oh . . . it is agony! The water is ice-cold and you feel that a sword is running down your arm. But you don't let yourself cry out . . . you brace yourself up, and with a sudden movement that is half a lunge and half a swoop you draw the scythe across. And if you are lucky, and cut clean, the reeds tremble for a moment and then fall, with their plumes stretching over the side of the boat.

Whereupon, you draw out your arm, which is stinging with cold, and pull the reeds towards you, arranging them in a pile on the floor of the boat.

§ I I I

There is something very sad about the fall of the reeds. But something beautiful too. For all the time, while you are reeding, you experience that strange exhilaration of the craftsman who is in *direct* contact with his work. Here are the reeds lying before you. They are the actual substance which is to provide you with a roof . . . and the provision of roofs is, after all, one of the major preoccupations of mankind. You, yourself, have found these reeds, which have been born of wind and water. And from wind and water they will protect you, till you are old, and die, and care neither for the wind nor for the rain.

Compare that occupation with the task of the average manual labourer, sitting in his factory, and then ask yourself if the Industrial Revolution was not, perhaps, the greatest affliction that ever visited this earth. For the factory worker has no joy, nor pride, nor interest, even, in his work. He may be one of a thousand men who, between them, are turning out some exquisite fabric — but what is that to him? He doesn't even see the fabric, he plays no part in its design, he does not even handle a needle. All he does is to stand day in and day out before a great machine, which roars at him incessantly, while he feeds it with oil and wearily watches its whirring steel arms.

It is as though the modern worker were some hypnotized acolyte in the service of a bloody goddess, called Capital, who never sleeps, who never smiles, who roars incessantly with an iron throat, who will starve those who do not obey, and send to destruction, impartially, those who love her or hate her.

§ I V

For weeks, the side of the lane outside my cottage was piled high with reeds, and the garden was awhirl with little pieces of feathery leaf and plume. There was a terrible amount of mess, inside and out, but I didn't care, for some of the happiest hours of my life were spent with the thatchers.

I don't know whether it was most fun indoors or out. To stand in a bedroom and hear mysterious tappings on the ceiling, to see the plaster crack by an old beam, bulge, and fall heavily on to the waiting dust-sheet . . . to wait for the iron spike that slowly threaded its way through, to catch a glimpse of light as the blue sky filtered into the dark room . . . that was delightful enough.

But it was even more fascinating, I think, outside. You scrambled up the ladder, up and up, to the dizzy height of nearly thirty feet. And then you lay with your tummy on the warm reeds, athwart the ridge, marvelling at the strange way in which the cottage appeared to you from this altitude. Why, you never realized it was so enormous. Your bedroom is miles away. And these chimneys, from which a faint blue haze of heat is rising, are gigantic. The bathroom, you see for the first time, is a little crooked . . . the eaves project at an odd angle, which explains why you can never get a proper view of the laburnum tree while you are lying in your bath.

The whole quiet pageant of Huntingdonshire is visible from this roof. It is like a lovely scroll unfolded. There, far away, is the bluebell wood, with the chequered fields beyond. There, to the east, is the white spire of Conington Church . . . and the Great North Road is just visible, with its silly procession of cars, some hurrying north and some hurrying south. (I often wonder what would happen if all the people who were hurrying north were suddenly switched round and compelled to hurry south, with angry expressions. And vice versa. Would the world be very different? Would they, themselves, be very different, even?)

However, that is getting us back to Pascal and his quiet room, and we must not look back, but forward.

§ v

It was not till the thatch was done that I began to take any serious interest in the accommodation upstairs. And the first thing I worried about was the bathroom.

Now, although I wanted to improve my bathroom, I did *not* want a 'super-bathroom,' especially at Allways. I have never understood the recent passion for rich, repressed women to pour their superfluous emotions into their bathrooms. I remember being shown over the house of such a one, not long ago. The house was a delicious square Georgian house in Hampstead . . . down a cul-de-sac, with enormous chestnut trees round the court, hanging the spring airs with their white candles, which the London winds blew to a sweeter flame.

We walked through this poor tortured house, with dreadful little squinting modern statues glaring at us from Sheraton alcoves. We walked up a staircase with glass banisters . . . '*So* amusing . . .' panted my hostess. (Lord, how I hate that word 'amusing'!) And after a number of doors had been opened, and we had observed white rooms, with cactuses, and yellow rooms, without cactuses, and green rooms, that looked like an immense cactus, with a prickly bed in the middle, we were privileged to witness the hostess's bathroom. It was done entirely in yellow glass. Yellow glass on the ceiling, yellow glass on the walls, yellow glass on the floor. And she said, with a roguish smile:

'I can see myself in sixteen different places, when I'm sitting in this bath.'

'I didn't know women *had* so many places,' I replied, remembering the exquisite wit of another lady.

And I am not asked to that house any more.

§ VI

Though I did not want a super-bathroom, I wanted an efficient one. I thought, until the Great Drought, that I had it. The water all had to be pumped up from the well into a little cistern under the roof, but the well had never failed. One only had to be a little careful of the water.

It was lovely brown water, as soft as silk, that plashed out of an ancient tap into a tiny white bath that lay in a corner under the eaves. I always had very small but efficient baths, in which one did a lot of soaping and wriggling to get the best effect. But my guests were not quite so considerate, which accounts for the following sort of conversation which has frequently echoed under the roof of Allways.

We are retiring for the night, having settled who wants what, and when, for breakfast. (It makes no difference by the way, what they say. The result is always eggs and bacon, at nine, in dressing gowns.)

Myself: *Do* have a bath in the morning, won't you?

Guest (somewhat startled): Why . . . yes. (And then

adds coldly, as though suspecting an accusation of uncleanliness). Thank you very much.

Myself: I should hate you not to have a bath.

Guest (emphatically): So should I.

Myself: It's just that all the water has to be pumped . . . so if you wouldn't mind *very* much not filling it *quite* to the top?

At this the guest usually enters into the spirit of the thing. Some guests even say that they will go so far as only to wash 'bits' . . . a statement that causes us to look away from each other, hastily. I urge them to wash every bit, but only, if they don't mind, not to lie in the bath with the water running indefinitely.

In the morning they usually forget, and I hear them lying in the bath with the water roaring out in torrents. This means that I have to go outside the door and clear my throat very loudly and bang suit-cases about. Whereupon the tap is quickly turned off, and a dead silence intervenes. The guest comes down to breakfast looking very clean but very guilty.

§ VII

And then, one day during the Great Drought, I turned on the tap, and nothing happened except a noise that is best spelt 'Hich' — the sort of noise that an angry Persian makes when some fool disturbs its most important meditations. I listened with dismay to this 'Hich,' turned and turned the tap, frowned at it, and then ran downstairs.

I found S. in the kitchen garden, pulling up dead broad-beans.

'I say, S., I've turned on the tap in the bathroom, and nothing happens.'

S. looked at me gravely, deposited a bundle of broad-beans on the parched earth, and accompanied me to the house.

And there we found the hideous truth. The well had run dry.

Yes . . . my little well, which I had always regarded as a sort of widow's cruse, perpetually to be replenished by the kindly gods of the underworld, had run dry. We opened the lid, and stared down into depths that were cool and dark, but dry as the desert.

Now do you see why I said that the drought was the cause of great events at Allways? For it was the sudden failure of my well which was the cause of my coming into intimate contact with the rest of the inhabitants of Allways. So we will break off here, for a moment, with the vision of those cool sad depths before us. And we will pay a few calls.

CHAPTER X

WOMEN AND WATER

I WISH that I had Trollope's genius for laying the map of
a village before you — quietly, clearly, with sweet and
homely words, so that you know just where the vicarage
gate is, and can mark, to a foot, the spot in the lane
where you must stand to get the best view of the church
spire. Such gifts being denied me, I can only draw a
rough sketch, where he would have painted a masterpiece.

The village of Allways is shaped like a capital S, and
its principal inhabitants are thus distributed in its
gentle curves:

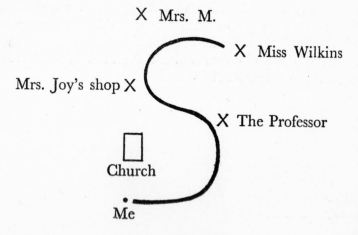

If that chart conveys anything whatever to you, I am
delighted. It really is accurate. For if you start from my

cottage, you take a bend to the right, and pass the church (and on summer evenings it is very difficult to pass because the setting sun turns all the windows to sheets of gold). Then a little farther on you come to a delicious white cottage on the right, which belongs to the Professor. I always associate the Professor with madonna lilies, because a bed of them runs all round his walls. I see them beginning to hoist their green belfries above the earth in spring; I watch their spires ascend through April and May; I see the bells being hung in June; and on quiet evenings I wander past, night after night, waiting for the bells to open and chime their scented praise to God . . . First one bell opens, and rings a hesitant note, then another . . . till there comes a day, towards the end of the month, when they are all pealing their chorus in the breeze and the whole village is drunk with a perfumed melody. Yet always, through the lighted window, I can see the Professor's head bent over his work, as though he had no time for the lilies.

We go on, and the next point of interest is Mrs. Joy's shop, which deserves a chapter to itself, and shall have it, if we ever get the time.

After that we come to the two ladies who are most active in our village life — Miss Wilkins, who lives in a lovely Tudor cottage at the extreme end of the village, and Mrs. M., who occupies The Hurst, beyond the village, with a private drive, beautifully gravelled, a large and scrupulously neat garden, and about fifty acres of the surrounding fields.

§11

We have already caught a glimpse of Mrs. M., in the opening chapter of this book. We left her striding down the lane with her abominably well-bred terrier, having been baffled in her efforts to find out what I was going to order for the kitchen.

Well, during that first year she continued to make inquiries, to be put off, and to be enraged by the manner in which, contrary to all her prophecies, I managed to hold out at the cottage, devoid of feminine aid, without starving, or developing chills from damp sheets. During the reign of Mrs. Wrench, it is true, she enjoyed certain minor triumphs.

But after the advent of the S.s she drew a blank, in spite of the most assiduous efforts.

'This is delicious trout,' she would say, on days when she came to dinner. It *was* delicious — beautifully jellied, and proudly emblazoned with a curly design of cream. 'I suppose you brought it up from London?'

'Oh no, Mrs. M.,' I replied, quite truthfully, 'Mrs. S. did it.'

'Really?' Mrs. M. glared at the trout as if it had bitten her. Then she forced herself to smile. 'So nice to think she always makes a special effort when I come.'

'But she doesn't make a special effort, Mrs. M.' I was so irritated that I did not pause to think that this was a somewhat discourteous remark. 'This is what we always have.' Then I added 'During the trout season,' because the argument seemed to be getting confused.

'In that case, Mrs. S. ought to be at the Savoy,'

snapped Mrs. M. However, she devoured her trout, and asked for more.

Usually, I violently resented Mrs. M.'s efforts to interfere in my household affairs. But there are disasters in life which make one forget all prejudices. The drying up of my well was such a disaster.

True, on the day after I made that terrible discovery, there was a violent thunderstorm, which lasted all night. When we woke up, the water-butts were filled to overflowing, and the well, once again, had four feet of water in it. But the thunderstorm was only a momentary relief in a rainless month. June went by, without a whisper of rain, and July marched on with hot and dusty feet. And the well sank lower and lower.

We got a can and tied a rope to it and sunk it into the well. Three feet of water only. On the following Sunday there was only two feet and seven inches. On the Sunday after that, a bare two feet! And the sky was as dry as a brass gong, with no sign that the thunder was going to beat its mammoth fists against it.

So one day I rose from the ground, where I had been lying on my stomach, looking into the well, dusted the dirt from my trousers and said 'I shall go and ask Mrs. M. about this. She knows everything.'

Now Mrs. M., needless to say, has the best well in the neighbourhood. Why the water should choose to flow so plentifully beneath her garden, I do not know. It just does. She had a well bored to eighty feet, and she gets as much as five hundred gallons an hour, when the little donkey engine which pumps it out is working at full speed. Moreover it is clear sparkling water — a little hard, but quite pure, like its owner.

I found Mrs. M. sitting in the garden, fanning herself, a large jug of the aforesaid water by her side.

'This heat!' she said, offering me some water, which I declined. 'I feel tempted to put in a swimming-pool.'

'That's just what I came to see you about Mrs. M.'

'What — a swimming-pool?' She spoke rather sharply, as though I were trying to push her into one against her will.

'No — the subject of water generally. My well seems to be drying up.'

A look of scarcely-veiled delight came into Mrs. M.'s eyes.

'Ah!' she said, 'I was always afraid that would happen.'

'You never *said* so, at any rate.'

'I never liked the look of that well of yours.'

'But you haven't even seen it, Mrs. M.!'

'One doesn't need to see it,' said Mrs. M., with infuriating loftiness. 'One only has to know a little about the lie of the land.'

'Well — what is the matter with the lie of my land?'

'Everything.' Mrs. M. sipped a glass of her hateful water. She sipped long and deliberately, as though she were trying to tantalize me with the thought of that abominable five hundred gallons an hour. 'You're *sure* you won't have some?' Then, loathsomely refreshed, she sat up, and fixed her gimlet eyes upon me.

'I always thought your well would dry up,' she said, in the brightest tones.

'I do think you might have . . .'

'Oh but *really*! It was hardly my place to do so, was it? As long as you were happy . . . .'

'But if you can have all the water you want, why can't I? We're on practically the same level, aren't we? It's the same soil, isn't it?'

And then Mrs. M., with one of her rare flashes of poetry, delivered a little homily on the subject of water. She did not mean to be poetical. She only wanted to 'stick to the facts.' But those facts. . . .

§ III

Have you ever realized the wild romance of the underground streams that run their errands, like a strange secret society, beneath the bland and unsuspecting fields of England? You are walking over a little hill in summer. The grass at your feet is dry and brown. The soil is parched. There are great cracks in the footpath — cracks where even the dandelions can hardly find a hold, and the common field daisies hang drooping heads. Yet, beneath your feet, perhaps only a few feet, perhaps only coffin-deep, there is a rill of sparkling water, that runs on and on, through the centuries, unseen, unheard.

You don't know it is there. Maybe, till the whole earth is dry, and floats through the winter of Infinity like a withered leaf, nobody will ever know about this little stream. Or one day, a man will come with a hazel-twig, and something will leap in the heart of the little stream, and the waters will surge up, excitedly, for a moment, while he stands above, in the sunny air, the twig twitching in his hands. We don't know. Meanwhile the stream runs on, whispering its secrets to the cool earth.

Oh — there is poetry in pools, and in lakes, and in the

rivers that run over the face of the earth. And there is infinite poetry, even, in a water-butt, which holds its dark, homely mirror to a sky that is always pleased to see its own image . . . a sky which looks prettier in this damp, weedy frame than through the roving eyes of an unhappy man. The man who cannot dream over a water-butt is to be pitied, for here is a mirror where life is kinder than outside — the blossom of the apple tree has a less piercing beauty, its challenging pinks flaunt themselves less arrogantly, take on a kindlier, dimmer hue in the shadow of the water. And at night, when the owls are hooting, if your eyes are sore with the blaze of stars, and your mind is dizzy with this drunken display of eternity above you, it is good to go out and feel the cool sides of the water-butt, and look down at the water, where these great mysteries are to be seen in miniature.

But the underground streams . . . these silver cords that have been threaded beneath the garment that is England . . . those are the waters that I love the best.

§ I V

Mrs. M. was saying:

'Water's a very funny thing. Underground water, I mean. Look at old Lady Thompson, at Yaxley. She had a water-diviner over from Lincoln. He went out in her garden with the hazel-twig, and the twig almost went mad, over her cabbage patch. By the way that twig went on, you'd think there was Niagara Falls just underneath her cabbages. So she told them to bore a well. They bored and bored and bored. They got down to a

hundred and forty feet. It was as dry as a bone. There
wasn't a drop of water . . . not a drop! And that little
experiment cost her two hundred pounds.'

'But she *has* got a well,' I said.

'Yes — but not where the water-diviner told her. Her
well's a good fifty yards away. And they only found it by
accident . . . when they were digging the foundations
of her new greenhouse. They'd only gone down five feet
when they struck water. And now she's got all she wants.
More than she wants, in fact,' added Mrs. M., 'because
water doesn't seem to be a drink she's very fond of, if
one's to believe all one hears.'

Having launched this poisoned dart in the direction
of the unsuspecting Lady Thompson she rose to her
feet and said 'Now let's come along and have a look at
this well of yours.'

We went through the house, which was deliciously
cool, with piles of pot-pourri in silver bowls, and
mahogany furniture so brightly polished that it would
have served as a looking-glass. Before going out of the
front door Mrs. M. gave final injunctions to her maid,
sotto voce:

'The pickle should simmer till *six*.' I heard . . . and
also 'I can have the leg devilled.' This remark greatly
pleased me. It is always nice to know what other people
are having for dinner, and it would be very satisfactory
to be able to think of Mrs. M. having her devilled leg
while I was having my chop. Of such small delights is
country life composed.

Our plan was to go straight to my cottage. But as we
were walking past Miss Wilkins's cottage, a head appeared
from over the hedge crowned with a fantastically rural

hat, from Bond Street, and underneath the hat was Miss Wilkins herself.

'Oh, my dears . . .' she cried '*What* heat! Poor me — exhausted! You're not going for a walk!'

'No,' said Mrs. M. 'We're not.' She said it rather shortly, and began to move on.

'Mrs. M. is going to help me with my well,' I said, apologetically.

'Your well?' Undine clapped her hands. 'Oh how divine! That's just what I want to-day. A quite enormous well with masses of icy water. I'll come too!'

I looked at Mrs. M.

'The well isn't dug yet,' said Mrs. M. 'At least the new one isn't. And really I don't think it would interest you.'

But Undine was already at the gate. 'It would enthral me,' she gurgled. 'There's nothing I like better than wells — dug or not dug. Water's so *exciting*. . . .'

'It is if you haven't got it,' snapped Mrs. M.

Undine ignored her. 'You must put a gargoyle on the top of your well,' she said to me, 'like mine. I call him my Water God. Whenever I drink a glass of water I think of him. And I've got a little reproduction of him in my bathroom. You *must* come and see. . . .'

'Are you coming?'

I longed to see Undine's bathroom, but I did not dare disobey Mrs. M. So I said I would love to, some day, but that we had to go on.

Undine called out that she would be with us in five minutes, after she had powdered her nose. She then disappeared through her door, singing an elaborately impromptu aria.

'Really!' hissed Mrs. M., as we walked down the lane. 'I've never heard such outrageous lies! She never touches a *drop* of Allways water.'

'How do you know, Mrs. M.?'

'Because her tool-shed is stacked from top to bottom with empty bottles of Vichy. It arrives in a crate at the station every month. I've often seen it when I go up to London.' She snorted. And then added hastily 'One can't help seeing addresses on packing-cases some-times.'

Mrs. M. is one of those people who prowl round other people's luggage at the station, surreptitiously lifting a label, and thinking dark thoughts about the people to whom the luggage is addressed.

'Why . . .' she went on, 'she doesn't even *pretend*, when one goes to lunch with her. There's always a bottle of Vichy there on the sideboard, for anybody to see. Of course, it *might* be filled with ordinary water.' Mrs. M.'s eyes gleamed for a moment at the thought of Undine filling Vichy bottles out of the tap. But the gleam faded. For why, if she filled the bottles with rain-water, should she continue to receive crates of Vichy from London?

She shook her head. 'No . . .' she observed. 'I don't think she'd descend to that!'

'But she really does seem to like rain water, Mrs. M., don't you think? To wash in, I mean?'

Mrs. M. spoke quite loudly. 'Then why doesn't she wash in it?'

'Mrs. M.'

'Why does she plaster her face with powder, and why does she have sixty-seven bottles of astringent lotion on her dressing-table? Rain water, indeed! If it ever rained on *her* face, it'd crack!'

By this time we were at the cottage. We met the gardener outside the kitchen door.

'Good afternoon,' said Mrs. M. 'I've come to look at this well of yours.'

For the next three minutes I heartily admired Mrs. M. She bent down, tugged the lid off, and stared into the depths.

'How many feet is there in there now?'

'Two and a half feet, madam.'

'How many feet after a heavy rain?'

'About five, madam.'

'Never higher?'

'No.'

There was a rapid fire of questions, in the same style. Mrs. M. turned to me. 'This is how I'd judge the situation,' she said. 'You aren't on a spring. Your water just filters in. It's not likely to dry up entirely, but you'll never have much to spare.'

'What ought I to do?'

'You should pump this well dry to-night, make a note of the time that it's dry, and then see what the level is in the morning. I prophesy it will be about four inches only, after twelve hours.' (This prophecy was accurate to half an inch). 'After that . . .'

However there was no time to issue further injunctions, for we heard La Belle Undine's voice from the distance. Willy nilly, we had to go and join her on the lawn.

'Let's dig a lovely hole here and it'll come up in fountains!' she cried, dancing round the lawn when she saw us.

'That's the last place to dig,' said Mrs. M. shortly. 'This is blue clay. You'll only find water in gravel veins.'

Undine shuddered. 'How frightful that sounds . . . gravel veins.' Then she fluttered to me again. 'Don't you think we could *induce* the water to come here? Supposing we sang to it . . . or danced?'

And then, without any warning, she began to warble the song which begins:

> 'My heart is like a singing bird,
> Whose nest is in a water-shoot . . . .'

I think those *are* the words. They seem incredible, but I am almost certain that those *are* the words which Christina Rossetti, in an eternally regrettable moment, committed to paper. And after this lapse on her part, some composer, of whose name I am unaware, discovered the words, and licked his lips, and made a terrible little gushing tune to fit them.

Since which date an endless procession of damp mezzo-sopranos have ogled their way on to the concert platforms of British provincial towns and chanted, with many gestures . . .

> 'My heart is like a singing bird
> Whose nest is in a water-shoot!'

So warbled Undine as she capered round the lawn. She rolled her r's in a very professional manner, even in the word 'water', which she made to sound almost Scottish. She could not remember the rest of the words, so she merely hummed the tune, and gestured with her arms.

'You'd better not do that near the well,' snapped Mrs.
M., 'or you'd fall in.'

'I'd *adore* to fall in on a day like this,' observed the
unsquashed Undine. She threw me a look. . . .
'Would you dive in and rescue me?'

This sort of question embarrasses me dreadfully. How
does a man answer it? Does he throw out his chin and
square his shoulders and say, 'Trust *me*, little girl?'
Or does he just smirk and cast down his eyes and draw
patterns with the toe of his shoe? Or does he, too, throw
the questioner a Look, as though he certainly *would*
rescue her, but would first take appalling liberties with
her, at the bottom of the well?

Mrs. M. saved the situation by saying:—

'If he did dive in he'd be a fool. There's only thirty
inches of water. So unless he hit you, he'd bump his
head on the bottom. And then there'd be two of you
to drag up.'

Undine looked at Mrs. M. coldly. 'How *lovely* to have
such a literal mind,' she remarked.

What would have happened if we had continued to
argue, I cannot imagine. But the situation was saved
by the sudden advent of the Professor, walking across
the lawn.

§ v

He had come to ask me a question about something,
but, as usual, he had forgotten what it was. For as he
had been walking through the garden, he had met S.,
who had taken him to the well, and told him all about
its drying up. He had also told him that we thought of

getting a water-diviner to see if it would be any use to sink a new well anywhere.

'Your man tells me you believe in witchcraft,' said the Professor abruptly, blinking at Mrs. M., and taking out of his pocket an envelope on which he made a small note.

(This, you must remember, is an incurable habit of the Professor's. Mrs. M. has never got used to it. She always thinks he is making notes about *her*.)

Mrs. M. straightened her hat nervously.

'Witchcraft?'

'Water-divining is witchcraft, isn't it?'

Mrs. M. broke in. 'Don't you believe in it?'

'I don't know. I believe in witchcraft, naturally.'

'Oh but you must believe in water-divining,' gurgled Undine. 'It's heavenly! You dance about with a lovely branch, and suddenly the branch dances too, and water comes up in *fountains!*'

The Professor did not reply. He merely blinked at Undine, took an envelope out of his pocket, and made another note. This damped Undine, for the moment.

He turned to me abruptly.

'Will you get a water-diviner? I'd like to test him.'

'Why, of course . . . .'

'Shall we say next Tuesday, after lunch?'

'Yes.'

The Professor blinked again, made another note, and then, with a sigh, turned on his heel and began to walk away. Suddenly he turned and came back. . . . .

'Oh, I've remembered what it was I wanted to say to you,' he said.

'Yes.'

'It's about flowers. I think some flowers are wicked.'

'Which flowers?'

'I don't mean any particular species. I mean individual members of the species. It's obvious, isn't it?'

Apparently my countenance was not beaming with intelligence, for he explained, a little impatiently:

'There are good men and bad men, aren't there? I mean morally good and bad. There are also good animals and bad animals. Some monkeys, for example, are definitely malicious and cruel and selfish. Others are just the opposite. It's the same with dogs. All down the scale. Even with fish. Don't you see? You've got a complete curve running down from man to the lowest animals. Why should it stop there? Why shouldn't it continue with the vegetable kingdom? I'm convinced it *does*.'

He walked over to a large sunflower that was flaunting itself in the border, blinked, shook his head at it, and departed.

Mrs. M., as soon as he was out of sight, tapped her forehead. But I believe there is something in what the Professor said.

CHAPTER XI

MAGIC

ON the evening before the water-diviner came, I
went round to see the Professor at his cottage. I found
him sitting in a room that smelt strongly of Flit. Even
as I was shown in to the room, by the giggling little
village girl who looks after him, he dashed to the
window with the Flit spray and squirted it violently five
or six times.

'Wasps?' I said, wondering how much Flit it would
take to suffocate a human being. Not much more than
the Professor was using, I imagined.

'No — moths.' He stared at the floor, and squirted
once more. 'I think that's finished it,' he sighed. 'I
have a horror of moths.'

'I know.'

'I could probably be psycho-analysed out of it, because I know exactly why I've got it. My father was a
brute. He used to ill-treat my mother. My room was
next to theirs, when I was a boy. I used to hear things,
through the wall. I couldn't sleep. I used to turn on
the light and stare out of the window . . . listening. And
the moths came to the window, and danced and danced
in the light. I never see a moth without hearing a
woman crying.'

He blinked, took out the inevitable envelope, and
made a note.

He said, 'Do help yourself to some sherry.'

He waved his hand to an empty decanter which was always kept among a mass of scientific apparatus on one of his tables. As long as I have known the Professor there has never been any sherry in that decanter. I am quite certain that he does not realize that it is empty. Perhaps this is due to the fact that whenever I am asked by him to have a glass of sherry, I politely step over to the table, and lift the empty decanter. By the time I have sat down again the Professor has forgotten all about it, and has plunged into the topic which is absorbing him for the moment.

It was so that evening. For he began to talk about water-divining without any further delay.

'It is obvious,' he said, 'that this influence, if it exists, is electrical.'

'Why?'

He blinked at me, impatiently. 'Because there is no contact between the water and the person holding the twig. That's why I call the influence electrical.'

'I should call it magic.'

'Magic *is* only another word for electricity. Now, since we know that we cannot send an electric current, of any power, through the ether, without a conductor, it must be only a slight current. One that you could cut off by spreading an insulator over the ground. That's the first experiment I should like to try on your water-diviner . . . to make him stand on a rubber bath-mat.'

'That would be grand,' I said. 'What else would you make him do?'

'I should ask him questions. I should ask him, for example, in what other parts of his body, apart from his hands, he felt this strange influence. If he was an honest man, I know what he'd answer.'

'What?'

'He'd tell me that he felt it on his tongue. Haven't you ever put a little toy battery to your tongue, and felt the sharp, bitter taste? Yes? Well, why do you feel that? Because your tongue is intensely sensitive. You feel as if the two little arms of the toy battery had been dipped in lemon juice. That's what a water-diviner ought to feel . . . if he's honest.'

'You *must* ask him that question,' I said. 'And what else would you like to do?'

'I *would* like,' said the Professor dreamily, 'to enclose his hands in plaster of Paris. And then to transmit a high frequency current through him. However, he'll probably be a country man. And if he were to see sparks coming out of his fingers, and possibly his nose, he might be alarmed.'

'I'm quite sure he would,' I said nervously. 'I don't think I should do anything like that, if I were you.'

'I shan't,' said the Professor. 'I shall bring along my apparatus, make some experiments, and compare my conclusions with those of the water-diviner. And if sparks come out of anybody's fingers, they'll come out of mine.'

We talked for some time about the approaching experiment. I was interested to learn that the Professor proposed to try the hazel-twig idea himself.

'But I shan't use a hazel-twig,' he said. 'I shall use a piece of copper wire. I haven't made up my mind about this business, one way or the other, but I *have* made up my mind about the hazel-twig. That is sheer superstition.'

Before I went he made one remark which filled me with misgiving. He said:

'If a water-diviner is to obtain any really valuable results, he must obviously be in a condition of complete tranquillity. He must be mentally at rest . . . susceptible to the most delicate influences.'

'Yes,' I said doubtfully.

But how were we to obtain this happy condition? For both Undine and Mrs. M. had made arrangements to 'call' on the following afternoon, in order to witness the proceedings. And the effect they usually had upon the Professor was far from soothing.

§ 11

My fears were more than justified.

The Professor arrived early, in his car. He brought with him two large boxes, that looked to my untutored eye like portable radios.

(I humbly apologize for the vagueness of my attempts to describe these scientific things. It must be maddening to anybody who knows anything about them.)

However, before making his experiments, the Professor wanted to wait for the water-diviner, who had not yet arrived.

'I do not propose to make him a present of any information I may obtain,' he said. 'Besides, I wish to see if I obtain any influences myself.'

He dragged from his pocket a piece of copper wire, and held it in front of him, gripping it firmly.

We were standing on the edge of the little wood, which was where I hoped that water would be found.

I saw that the Professor was about to go into a sort of trance, and I prayed that he might get it all over before the arrival of Undine and Mrs. M. But at that exact moment there was the sound of a creaking gate, and both these ladies made their appearance. Undine was tremulous with excitement. Mrs. M. looked grim and efficient. I observed that she was carrying a forked hazel-twig in her left hand. So *she* was going to see if she could find water, too! That was all really very unfortunate.

Meanwhile the Professor was rapidly going into his trance. He was stepping forward slowly, holding the copper wire between his hands, and looking up to the sky. I turned round to the approaching ladies, trying to warn them not to disturb him. But it was too late. Undine cried out:

'Oh, Professor . . . let *me* . . .' She tripped up to him. . . . 'Do let *me!*' She stood in front of him, pleading.

The Professor blinked. The copper wire dropped from his hands.

'Hell!' said the Professor, softly but very clearly. And then he picked up the copper wire and strode away angrily to one of his boxes.

I bustled about. I appeased Undine, who was inclined to make a scene. I made faces at Mrs. M., and suggested that she would be best employed if she tried to find water before the diviner arrived . . . a suggestion which she endorsed heartily. She immediately hung up her bag on the palings, took the hazel-twig, and proceeded to wander about, followed by the contemptuous glances of Undine. Then I went to the Professor, and after a great deal of argument, induced him to return and resume his operations.

He returned, and once more took out the piece of copper wire. I watched him anxiously. Would he go into a trance? Would the wire jump all over the place? Would Undine behave herself?

The Professor's face did not look at all trance-like. It grew more and more irritated. And to my dismay I saw that his eyes were fixed, not on the heavens, but on Mrs. M., who was making wide circles round us with her hazel-twig.

The Professor dropped his hands. 'It is hopeless,' he said.

'But really . . .'

'You do not understand.' He drew his hand wearily over his eyes. 'To be completely receptive to an extremely delicate influence such as this, one must be in a condition of peace. And at the moment — (here his voice rose sharply) — at the moment I am *not* in a condition of peace.'

There was an awkward silence. Undine, whose personal affront had been forgotten in a common hostility to Mrs. M., breathed a sympathetic . . . 'poor *darling* Professor . . .' but quickly subsided when he darted a look at her that was as withering as a flash of lightning.

Mrs. M., meanwhile, continued to frisk around with her hazel-twig, like a large and irritating bird with a worm in its beak. And all the time she was making 'tut tut' noises, as the twig failed to respond. Now and then, she would pause for a second, and the twig would twitch. But it soon stopped, and she shook her head, said 'tut tut,' and frisked off again.

Now all these antics were obviously done with an eye on the gallery. Mrs. M. knew very well that we were watching her. And so, in order to taste to the full this agreeable publicity, she came much closer to us and remained standing a few yards away, with the twig twitching, ever so slightly . . .

'Couldn't you . . . couldn't you try once more, Professor?' I ventured.

'No!' His voice rasped out, very loudly.

'What *is* disturbing you, Professor?' asked Undine, knowing very well that the cause of the whole trouble was Mrs. M.

'Somebody,' boomed the Professor, 'is sending out emanations.'

I do not know why this remark should have made us both feel so very shy, but it did. It is highly embarrassing to be told that somebody in the company is sending out emanations. Each person in the company feels, in a way, suspect. And so both Undine and I glared at Mrs. M., as though to say, 'Well, if anybody has emanated, it wasn't *me!*'

But the Professor had by far the most powerful eye. And since he was casting a look of sustained hatred at Mrs. M., who had distinctly heard his remark, she suddenly realized the charge that was being levelled at her. She dropped her hazel twig and advanced towards us.

'Professor!'

'I am sorry,' observed the Professor, 'but it is necessary for me to tell the truth.'

'And to make insulting remarks?'

'Insulting?' The Professor's eyes were really blazing now. 'Why is it insulting to tell you that you have a strong personality?' He took a step forward. 'To tell you that you *disturb* me?'

Mrs. M. took a step backward. This was a development for which she was entirely unprepared.

'But . . . but . . .'

'Disturb me!' repeated the Professor, angrily.

'But surely . . . if I don't talk . . . and remain quite still?' Mrs. M.'s voice had a pleading tone, but I could detect in it a faint echo of arrogance — the arrogance of a woman who knows she is 'disturbing.'

'It would make no difference,' said the Professor. Then an idea struck him . . . 'Wait a minute!'

'Yes?' Mrs. M. looked at him eagerly.

'Your head!' cried the Professor. 'Yes . . . we can enclose your head in a network of copper gauze!'

'What!'

This remark was so very unexpected that for a moment nobody could do anything but stare at the Professor. The corners of my mouth were twitching spasmodically, but I was saved from actual laughter by the fact that the vision of Mrs. M.'s head in a veil of copper gauze was not merely funny, it was a little terrifying. Those cold, hard features . . . the humourless mouth . . . the anxious eyes . . . staring through a mist of metal. . . .

There was no time to remonstrate with the Professor. For he was off again.

'And then,' he said eagerly, 'you should get some quite sexless person to hold your hand — somebody without the least trace of . . .'

158

He turned round and held out his hands to Undine. What would have happened at that moment if he had been allowed to continue, I do not know. I think that we should all have left Allways and emigrated to foreign parts. But just as the Professor was making his dreadful gesture to Undine, there was a whir of wheels in the lane outside, and a grinding of brakes, and the sound of a slamming door.

There were footsteps across the gravel. And a man with curious eyes stood in front of me and announced himself as the water-diviner.

§III

The next hour was one of the most interesting that I ever spent.

The Professor, fortunately, was so absorbed in the new arrival that he quite forgot Mrs. M. and Undine. He stared very hard at the water-diviner (who was called by the agreeable name of Sparkler) and constantly took out his envelope to make notes about him. I could not help thinking how awful it would be if Mr. Sparkler accused the Professor of sending out 'emanations.' However, he didn't. He only smiled. And his eyes twinkled. They were enormous eyes that somehow reminded one of clear water. They were not 'watery.' They were just very liquid, and faintly shot with green.

He took the twig from his pocket and looked straight ahead of him. Then he began to walk. He walked very slowly with his arms rigid to his side. We trooped after him.

'Does this take it out of you?' I said.

He nodded. It was as though he found it difficult to speak.

A hush descended on us as we followed him through the long grass. There was no sound save the swish of the grass against our ankles, and the heavy breathing of the water-diviner. I felt a slight tingling in my skin . . . there was something queer about all this, as though one were at a séance. At any moment, it seemed, a cloud might drift across the sun, and a chill wind blow over the meadows, and from the air above there might come the wail of unearthly voices.

'Oh . . . oh!'

It was Undine who cried out. For suddenly, right in the middle of the field, the hazel-twig had shot up in the hands of Mr. Sparkler. It was as though it were wrenched by an unseen hand.

He turned round. He was panting and there was sweat on his forehead.

'You'll find water here, sir,' he said.

§ I V

I wish I could describe the next stages in the proceedings as scientifically as they should be described. But I can only draw pictures, where, I fear, I should be enumerating statistics.

Those pictures are vivid enough, however. I can see the Professor panting across the field, dragging a rubber bath-mat after him. I can see the look of astonishment on Mr. Sparkler's face when, standing on the bath-mat, over the exact spot where he had found the water, the twig refused to move. I can see the look of relief that

came over him when, the bath-mat having been removed, the twig jumped again. It was as though a man
who had been temporarily blinded were restored to
sight.

I can see, too, the hurryings and scurryings which
accompanied the Professor's own experiments, which
were conducted, now, in full view of a row of heads
belonging to the village boys who had heard that some
devilment was afoot (as usual) at Thatch Cottage, and
had hurried from the village green to glare, and make
purple remarks about the proceedings.

'Whoy's 'e puttin' in them somethin' pegs?'

'What's in them somethin' boxes?'

'Whoy's 'e puttin' 'is somethin' nose in the somethin'
box?'

'What the 'ell's that somethin' row? 'As 'e got a swarm
o' bees in that there box?'

Thus did they comment upon the Professor's activities.
I can't explain them. He told me he was 'measuring the
electrical resistance.' He also told me that one of his
instruments was 'percussive,' and was sending a tremor
through the ground. Mrs. M., who had heard this
remark, began to twitch violently, and complain of
shock, but the Professor snapped at her that she was
suffering from delusions.

Anyway, at last, after the boxes had clicked for an
interminable time, and an infinite number of calcula-
tions had been made on stray envelopes, the Professor
rose to his feet, walked across the field, glanced at his
envelope, turned to the right, and then suddenly thrust
his stick into the ground.

'You will find water here,' he said.

It was at the exact spot where the water-diviner's twig had twitched.

And we did. Clear, cold, sparkling water, at a distance of only fourteen feet.

When, a few weeks later, we came to dig the well, there was ten feet of water in it a few hours after we had reached the rocks which lay fourteen feet below the surface. And as far as I can see, this water is as inexhaustible as the widow's cruse.

So who was right? The man of science or the man of the soil? Where did the secret lie — in the Professor's boxes or in the throbbing wrists of the 'yokel'?

Does it matter?

I don't think so. No . . . I don't care at all when I lie in my bath, and turn on the tap, and revel in the magic waters that we have conjured up from the darkness below.

CHAPTER XII

LEAVES AT THE WINDOW

WE have now arrived at the second autumn. Every time the front door is opened the little calendar in the hallway flutters madly in a breeze that is sharpened with a hint of frost. The calendar marks:

OCTOBER IST

And then adds, in a sinister *sotto voce*:

'Pheasant shooting begins.'

What strange minds calendar-makers must have, I think, whenever I pass it. For them, something is always 'beginning,' and it usually begins with a bang. Or if it does not begin with a bang, it informs us that some distinguished person is having a birthday. It is almost impossible to open one's calendar without being reminded, either that some bloodthirsty man is loading his gun, or that some weary creature is dictating polite replies to ambassadors who have felicitated her on an event which she would infinitely prefer to forget.

I would like a calendar that drops subtler hints. I would like one that told me not to forget to go and look for spindle-berries in the wood, because already they will be stained pink, bringing the days of apple-blossom to the heart of winter. I would like to be reminded that there may still be a few mushrooms in the sheltered valleys — mushrooms that never grow very big but

163

are excitingly black underneath, and taste all the sweeter because you are only just in time to rescue them from the ground-frost. I would like to be told to order paper bags for the chrysanthemums, because if you put a nice big paper bag over the flowery crowns of your tall chrysanthemums you will never suffer the agony of seeing their golden petals tarnished at the edges. If you think it must be a bore to do this, I assure you that you are mistaken. Nothing is greater fun then going out in the morning, lifting off the paper bags, which are frozen stiff, and finding the brilliant, glowing flowers underneath. You can stand up the paper bags all the way down the path, and when they are all off you can squash them in your hands, with a delicious crinkling noise as you breathe the acrid sweetness of the grateful blossoms.

During that second autumn I was greatly exercised about this problem of sheltering the flowers outside. Some of them had to suffer, I knew. Nature must take her toll, and all that. But the little creepers by the house . . . the flowers that were nestling under the eaves . . . so near and yet so far. Could one not do something about *them?*

I was particularly worried by a grape-vine which I planted in the previous November. This was not the vine to which I referred in my previous chronicle of Allways. No — this was a new comer. It had been planted in a rose-bed in the secret garden, and was trained against the wall outside the Garden Room. The rose-bed was about three feet from the wall, and there was a path in between, so the vine had to take a flying leap over the path, and land on the wall, which it did extremely gracefully. As the path was a tiny cul-de-sac people did not walk up it, or they would have tripped over the stem.

All through the summer this vine produced grapes galore. However, very few of them had ripened before the first frost came and turned them brown. This is so bitter a memory to me that I hate to think of it.

'Why, oh *why* did the frost have to come just then?' I sighed; on the morning that it happened. 'And why, oh *why* didn't I know it was coming? I could have got an oil stove, or something, or a blanket.' It made me feel terrible to think that I had been sleeping, like a loathsome profiteer, wrapped in quantities of blankets, with the radiators filling my room with warmth, while the wretched vine had been stabbed to the heart by the cold arrows of the frost — the sweet bloom of its grapes rudely destroyed.

I stared at the vine, and as my regret grew more intense, so my brain began to work out little plans for next year. (It is always 'next year' when you have a garden.) And suddenly I realized that I had the germ of an idea. It developed from a wild thought that if one had only known, the stem could have been loosened from the wall, and the whole vine could have been trailed into the Garden Room for the night, if the window were left an inch open to allow the stem to pass through. I should have had to leave a note for the housekeeper, so that she would not stagger back in the morning under the impression that the vine had come to life, and was stalking through the house, seeking what it might devour. But that would have been a detail.

Seriously, was it so impossible? Here on the other

side of the wall was warmth and comfort. Only a few inches away. Was it beyond the ingenuity of man to bring some of that warmth and comfort to the vine?

It was not.

This was what we did. (It is terribly difficult to explain without a plan, but all the plans I have drawn look like soda-water syphons standing on a map of the battle of Waterloo, so it is better to stick to words.)

I summoned Mr. Joy and got him to build a long, coffin-shaped box. (He makes coffins, by the way, and complains bitterly that his nephews always spend his coffin-money on riotous living before he has time to put anything by for his old age.)

We bored two holes through this box, one at the side and one at the top, and then we took the box to the vine, threaded the stem through — (the box had to be cut in half, and put together again, but that is an unnecessary complication) — and set it against the wall.

The situation was then as follows: The end of the vine stem, where it plunged into the earth, was exposed, as it should be. But six inches up it entered the box, remained in the box for about two feet, and then emerged at the top of the box and proceeded to clamber up the wall.

The box was then painted white, so that it looked like a long garden seat, set against the wall, under the window.

And *then* . . . . I had grooves made along the edges of the box, got four large pieces of fabulously expensive glass, set the glass in the grooves and set another piece of glass on top. Then one had a little sort of greenhouse, which looked like an extra bay window, completely covering the vine.

I rushed into the house to see what it looked like from inside.

As soon as I opened the door I breathed a sigh of relief. You would not have known the glass was there. You just saw the original window, and the Secret Garden beyond.

I walked across to the window and opened it. Stretched out my hand. Tapped the glass. Stroked a leaf of the vine. Said to the vine: 'I'm terribly sorry I didn't think of this before. But next year. . . .'

§ 11

Next year, we were amply rewarded. The glass remained in place all through the winter, except during a very mild week when we removed it. (It only took about a minute and a half to slide the glass out of the grooves and prop it up against the wall.) And though you would never know that it was there, except when it was snowing, or raining, there was always the delightful consciousness that the vine was being protected, that it had become, as it were, a member of the family. On bitter grey days, in March, when the wind had the sting of a lash, I would open the window in the Garden Room and gloat over the tiny green buds that were already swelling on the vine. 'I wonder if you realize how spoilt you are,' I would say indulgently. The vine did not answer. 'I suppose you know' I went on, 'that even the Scotch firs are looking down in the mouth? That the Berberis Bealii is nipped to the bone? And that the Lonicera fragrantissima is a positive wreck?'

But though the vine did not answer, in words, it

answered, most lavishly, in deeds. For on the following summer, it had a good two months' start over the rest of the creepers. By the end of June its plentiful clusters had already begun to form. The glass had long been removed, of course, though the box-seat remained.

In the last week of July, when the grapes were black, I took great pleasure in leading people out to this seat, and asking them, carelessly, if they would not like to sit down for a moment.

'But grapes . . .' they exclaim.

'Grapes?' I say vaguely, looking in the wrong direction.

'But *masses* of grapes — out of doors — in July!'

'Oh *those*,' I say, unmoved. 'Yes. They really ought to be thinned out.'

'But how do you do it?'

Whereupon I sit down, blocking out the view of the tell-tale glass, which is only half concealed under a cascade of clematis.

'There is something very remarkable', I say, 'about the climate of Huntingdonshire.'

§ III

However, one could not build little glass-houses outside every window in the cottage. The vine happened to be ideally situated for such treatment. If one had tried it on other creepers, it would have looked ridiculous. And so, as far as that was concerned, I had to be content with protecting a few of the rarer winter flowers with sacking.

And every night, when I went to bed, I opened my

window, and gently lifted in a spray of wistaria, which had clambered up to the glass and was beating its frozen fingers on the pane.

There were, however, many other ways in which I succeeded in bringing the garden indoors.

One of them, of course, was with great baskets of everlasting flowers.

I do not think most people take enough trouble with their baskets of everlasting flowers. They stuff them in untidily, and half the flowers rot, and the whole affair is soon covered with dust, so that it reminds one of those gruesome collections of pampas grass and honesty and sea thistles which are arranged on the mantelpieces of seaside boarding houses, with the Black Prince, in bronze, on the left, and a view of Mont Blanc, with real frosting, on the right.

For the basis of my everlasting bunches I found, after the first year, that it was best to form a groundwork of statice rather than of the popular helichrysum. (That sounds very pompous, but statice, as you probably know, is sea-lavender, and helichrysum is the Sunday name for the ordinary 'everlasting' flower.) There are three sorts of statice which are absurdly easy to grow from seed — pink, yellow and mauve. You should pick them, the instant they are in flower, and dry them in the sun, because if you leave them too long on the plant the stalks will grow mouldy.

Nothing could be prettier than a basket which has a groundwork of these three shades of statice. (By the way, you want to sow about twice as much pink and yellow as mauve, if you wish to obtain an equal quantity.)

When you have your ground work you can add the everlasting flowers, to taste, and also a few sprays of that very delightful flower, which is not nearly well enough known, called xeranthemum. I never hear that word without thinking of a limerick which runs:—

We've got a new maid called Xeranthemum
Who said 'I've been living at Grantham, mum:
　　But my mistress took fright
　　For I snored in the night,
To the tune of the National Anthem, mum.

The xeranthemum is a most versatile flower with as many varieties of colour as the nemesia. You can sow it out of doors in April, and cut it in August, again remembering to cut it the moment it flowers.

There are only two other things I put in my everlasting bunches. One is obvious and the other is An Invention.

The obvious one is maidenhair fern. I do not know if it is very Philistine of me, but after cutting the sprigs of maidenhair, and after drying and pressing them, I dip them in green ink. Ordinary green ink at a penny a bottle gives them a beautiful grass green colour which lasts all through the winter.

The Invention — which *sounds* vulgar and hideous, but *is* gay and delightful — is feathers. Ordinary white hen's feathers, about four inches long, pushed in between the dry, rustling petals. They give just that touch of white which you cannot get in everlasting flowers. And they look like flowers themselves . . . you would not know they were feathers until you went close up to the basket.

Reading this over I seem to have given a detailed and touching description of How To Make A Hat That An Eccentric Female Could Wear In Church On Palm Sunday In The Year 1901. The sort of hat in which one could feel *really* thankful that King Edward had made such a speedy recovery from his operation for appendicitis.

Well, let us leave it at that. If you could see my little bowls and baskets, glowing in dark corners throughout the winter, by the side of a bed, on a window-ledge, in an empty space on a bookshelf, you would not laugh at them. Rather would you praise the gallantry with which they keep their sweet complexions even in the face of flaunting cinerarias and elegant cyclamens; that are like débutantes, dancing for their few days of life, while the well-preserved wallflowers watch them from the shadows. But no . . . the everlasting bunches do *not* remind me of wallflowers. They have an eternal youth. And if you take them to your heart, something of that youth will flow through their strange, dry petals into your own heart.

§ v

This is a book about a house, as we have said before, and it is not fitting, therefore, that we should deal here with the lore of bulbs, nor peer into the attics and cupboards to see if the Cynthella hyacinths are sprouting, nor inquire, querulously, why nearly all the winter, irises send up such deceptive fountains of green leaves without a single flower, like heralds that blow their trumpets flamboyantly for kings that never come.

Yet, as we are talking about bringing the garden indoors, I would like to tell you of one funny little experiment I made during this second winter at the cottage.

Flowers, I had, through the everlasting bouquets. And bouquets. And creepers, through the vine. And quantities of gloriously bronzed beech branches. (It seems almost impertinence on my part to remind you that if you wish to keep branches of bronze beech leaves all through the winter, you must plunge their stems in a mixture of half water and half crude glycerine. But there may be some small, depraved person, living in a damp cave somewhere, who does not know this vital fact. If so, I would ask the small depraved one not to forget to ask for *crude* glycerine. Why it is called *crude*, I do not know, because its results are most elegant, and will keep your beech leaves in perfect condition till spring is well on the way.)

My experiment was due to a sudden aching realization that though the flowers had been induced to walk, as it were, into the house, and the leaves too, and the vine, the *wood* had shown no signs of coming in. And I did so bitterly want an indoor wood. For weeks I toyed with the idea of a model Japanese garden, but the more I saw of model Japanese gardens the less I liked them. There was something a little uncanny about them . . . those stunted trees, whose roots must surely be tortured against the arty China in which they had usually been repressed. And those sinister little cactuses, and the even more sinister tin coolies, wandering over a bridge into a whirl of moss. What happened to those strange figures, when they crossed the bridge? Would they sink into the moss, or would they walk on and on, until they came to the edge? And having come to the edge would they have the decency to remember that they were only tin, or would they suddenly take on a hideous mimic life, and jump over, and crawl up the dinner table, and present themselves against one's wine-glass at awkward moments? That stork, too — that inevitable stork that is always to be found in Japanese gardens, glaring with an imbecilic expression at some dreary little water plant — I felt that that stork should not be encouraged. It had probably been produced by the hundred thousand in unhygienic factories in Yokohama, by men who burn widows with the utmost alacrity, and say *yam-yam*, and eat rice with a barge-pole, and then go out and burn some more widows. (That is all that Balliol ever taught me about Japan.)

No — I wanted something simpler. A *real* wood, indoors, with the tang of wet earth about it, and a sense of blowing branches. A wood over which the desolation of winter would brood, and the mists of spring would hover — a wood which in summer would cast its shade and in autumn its leaves.

It sounds an impossible ideal, when you remember that all these emotions had to be concentrated in a couple of square feet of pottery, which could be placed on a side table. Yet . . . it succeeded. The secret was beech-nuts.

§ VI

There are but few beech trees in Huntingdonshire. They do not take kindly to our particular brand of clay.

But here and there, in a valley, or alone in a far-flung field, you will find this lovely tree — this tree whose trunk, in winter, is gay with emerald moss, while the winds play their sweetest tunes in and out of its bleak choirs. Such a tree I found, and loved, that stood in solitude on the edge of the bluebell wood as if it had been sent to Coventry by the other trees, or as if it were too proud to join them. Often I would go and lie beneath this beech. I know it so well that the shadows must surely have thrown their pattern across my heart.

On this second autumn I was lying under the beech one day when I suddenly saw a tiny beech by my elbow. I sat up and saw another. And another. The whole ground was dotted with tiny beech trees. They never seemed to be more than a year old . . . something happened, apparently, after the first year. But at least they *did* seed themselves, and push their stems through the earth, and produce their little silky leaves, that were as green as the eyes of very small, very timid kittens.

Why not collect some beech-nuts, find the choicest possible soil, place them in a big earthenware bowl and see what happened? If the worst came to the worst they would only go to sleep. And meanwhile, one could recite poems over them, imploring them to make an effort, telling them that the world was waiting for them, that there was a very white ceiling hovering over them, and a golden-forked fire, leaping with excitement about them.

I filled my pockets with beech-nuts. When I returned, I chose twelve of the brownest, glossiest nuts I could find. Then I placed them, very gently, in an earthenware bowl filled with the softest earth. I did not water them.

I put them in a dark cupboard. And waited. And waited. And waited.

November came, with a canter of wild winds, and a scurry of sleet. December was silent, and awe-struck . . . one had a sense of a giant, hooded figure, brooding beneath a canopy of frozen stars. January was gay and absurdly spring-like. Birds sang. There were sheets of golden aconites under the elm. The snow-drops laughed all day long. Somebody had told them that life was hard and difficult, whereas they found it bland and easy and delightful. February stamped an iron foot on the snowdrops — stamped so sullenly and so long that the earth was like a sheet of iron, stiff with sorrow, and hardened against all adversity. March was tempestuous: there were days of snow and days of sun — black days and white days, flashing past in a fierce kaleidoscope . . .

April came.

I opened the door of the cupboard.

Twelve little beech trees got up and bowed.

You must forgive the dramatic licence. Needless to say I had opened the door of the cupboard a great many times before — so often, in fact, that the hinges were almost worn off. But it happened that I had to be away from the cottage for a whole month during the time that the little beech-nuts were making their last effort. And when I *did* open the door . . . there they were. All twelve of them. With leaves so tiny that it hurt. Of a green that baffles description. A green that is almost yellow, but with a magic that no yellow has ever attained in this world.

The beech trees flourished all through the year.

They are now three years old. They are about a foot high. They do all the right things. They respond most exquisitely to the seasons whose vagaries they only know by instinct. Yet, by the manner in which they burgeon in spring, and swell in summer, and flush in autumn, and despair in winter, you would say that they were outside the house, instead of in. It is as though they heard the call of the Seasons, as they marched by, as though the Seasons entered, and caressed them or ravished them, as the case may be. I hope it is like that. For they are brave and beautiful, and I love them.

M

The
Study

CHAPTER XIII

WHOOPS

AND now it is time to pay an apology.

Always, during these adventures, a black shadow has been at our side. Upstairs, downstairs, indoors and out, up every path, down every lane, sniffing into every cupboard, examining with the gravest interest every packing-case that has been undone, getting the last ecstasy of smell out of every mysterious parcel . . . this shadow has followed us.

He has been with us every moment of the day and I have not even introduced you to him. I am terribly sorry. Here . . . Whoops! Where *is* that dog? Ah — there he is. Rushing round the archway like a black tornado. Here — steady on! *Will* you get down? No, we are *not* going for a walk! Oh Lord — these trousers looked foul enough already and now there's a new layer of mud on them. *Will* you stay still for a moment? There, that's better. Now, this is Whoops.

What sort of a dog is he? Now, is that a very tactful question? Can't you see he is a quite unique sort of dog, with a style of his own? You do see that, but you can't make out *what* he is? Really, you shouldn't ask such questions. Dogs always know when they are being discussed, and it embarrasses them. Being essentially manly and British — I always feel that England is the spiritual home of all good dogs — they don't like

179

being discussed. Honestly, it isn't done, they say. And they slink off, with that terrible humility which dogs have, and sit under the table, and prop their chins on their paws, and look at you, more in sorrow than in anger, until you have remembered your manners again. You should always be much more careful about what you say in front of dogs than about what you say in front of people. Dogs understand the subtleties of language so much more acutely than men. You can't fool them with bright words when your throat is dry and your heart is aching.

But you still want to know *what* he is? All right. You had better hear the awful truth. Lean forward a bit. You didn't hear? Well . . . come closer. *He is a mixture between a poodle and a chow.*

All right. Laugh away. I don't care. Your own dog may be a terrier with sparks coming out of its back and legs like funnels and a pedigree as long as the last baby in the *Forsyte Saga*. Or it may be a Borzoi so well-bred that it has a brain like the remotest cousin of the most peculiar grand duke in the dustiest department of the Spanish nobility. Or it may be a frightful little thing from Germany that looks like a decayed ostrich feather, and swoons if it does not like the shade of the new footman's hair. You can keep your aristocratic dogs. Give me a mongrel.

What was that? A growl from under the table? Good Lord . . . I'd forgotten that Whoops was listening. We had better apologize quickly, because Whoops is really anything but a mongrel . . . . at least, I mean, his parents are of the highest standing. Here is his pedigree:

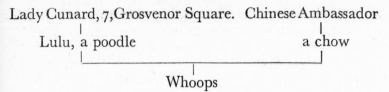

Whoops

Lulu was the largest, woolliest, most diabolically attractive poodle that the world has ever known. Long, long ago, when I used to go out to lunch parties, Lulu was the star attraction at the house of the bird-like Lady Cunard. When Lulu came into the room one forgot what Winston Churchill had been saying . . . one even forgot what George Moore had been saying . . . for Lulu was a contemporary of George Moore, with his same exquisite sense of style . . . of *le mot juste* . . . She timed her little guttural sneezes better than any dog I have ever known.

'Would you like one of Lulu's puppies . . . I think some seem to be coming?' said Lady Cunard one day, when Lulu was looking a little pensive, and was walking somewhat heavily round the drawing-room.

Would I like one of Lulu's puppies? There could be only one answer to such a question. From that moment, I became an anxious father. And when, eventually, the happy event occurred, it disturbed me not at all to find that Lulu's affections had been fickle . . . that she had broken caste, and had looked with a favourable eye upon the chow that sat, so impressively, on the steps of the Chinese Embassy.

For the result was adorable. A little black bundle of poodle, with a huge chow tail, arched over his back like a pennant . . . and yet a tail that was not quite sure of itself, liable to dejected trailings at the least harsh word. Eyes as large and as brown as any Irish colleen's. Finally, to show his romantic parentage, a jet-black tip to his pink tongue.

Now do you still laugh when you hear that he is a mixture of a poodle and a chow? No? You are quite right. For it is the best sort of dog any man could possibly have. In fact, I might almost give you the same reply as the bored young man who was asked whether he would drink champagne or 'some other wine.' '*Are* there other wines?' he replied, with raised eyebrows.

I can raise my eyebrows too. I can also ask '*Are* there any other dogs?'

§11

He was very frightened, very woolly, and very small on the day that I called at Grosvenor Square to fetch him. He followed the butler up the stairs, stood for a moment trembling, caught sight of me and dashed away again. This happened several times. Each time that he saw me he flew like the wind, and took refuge under the kitchen table, where he stayed, wagging his tail feverishly, but not at all happily, lifting one paw as though to shield himself.

I had hoped that he would follow me. But no! He had to be dragged towards me, sliding over the marble pavement as though he were being led to the slaughter. I bent down and stroked him. He was trembling violently. Then I put him on the lead . . . .

'Dog . . . .' I said softly, for he had no name . . . 'dog . . . please come along . . . we are going to the country . . . d'you hear? . . . to the country . . . grass and trees and hedges with rabbits in them. . . .'

But Whoops only looked round with an imploring expression at his friend, the butler, asking him when this misery would end.

At last I got him outside. We had about half a mile to walk to Berkeley Street, where the car was parked. It was so muddy a day that I could not carry him. He had to be half pushed, and half pulled. The pushing was easier than the pulling, because when he was pulled at all hard he spread out his four legs and slid, making terrible choking noises.

This was awful. Whoops was the first dog I had ever owned, and I was extremely anxious to be a success with him. But nothing I could do was any good. If I spoke to him he only put on an expression of frightful torture, slightly averting his head, and looking at me out of the corners of his eyes.

The streets were crowded, and the people who passed me on the pavement glared at me as though I were a child-murderer. 'Poor little dog' they said, audibly. 'It's a shame.' I began to grow purple in the face, looked round wildly for a taxi. None came. We crawled on, breathlessly, by inches. If it was possible for Whoops to entangle himself in a passer-by he did so. He would dart off to the side just as I thought we had established some sort of forward movement, and the lead would be stretched tight in front of some hurrying female, who had to leap into the air in order to avoid it. And all the time I had to force an agonized smile to my face and mutter things about 'just a puppy . . . going to the country . . . only had him to-day . . . terribly sorry.'

None of these remarks, obviously, were heard, but they served the purpose of making the people who were tripped up imagine that I was a dangerous lunatic, and thereby refrain from molesting me.

At last we reached the car. Ignoring the mud, I lifted Whoops up, and put him on the seat. He immediately scrambled off it, and cowered on the floor. I leant down to pat him, but it brought on such an access of trembling that I gave it up.

Sadly the car began to thread its way through the maze of streets that lead to the Great North Road. I felt depressed and humiliated. 'It would have been better', I said to myself 'to stick to cats.'

§ 111

Look upon that picture . . . and on this.

It is six months later and I am coming up for the week-end.

The car swerves through the country gate, into the wooden garage, and stops, in semi-darkness. I switch the engine off. For a moment there is silence. And then, there is a scurry over the gravel, and two shaggy paws pounce on the window ledge. They are immediately followed by a rough black face, from which shine great brown eyes, illuminated by an expression of rapture more fit to be lavished on angels than on men.

What has caused this amazing change? God knows. I had been no kinder to him than any other master would have been. I had just taken him round, and introduced him to the country, and told him not to be so silly and frightened . . . told him that the fat thrushes hopping about after worms would not hurt him, but that he should beware of the bees, whom he used to sniff so tenderly. I had taught him to come when he was called, and to stay at my heels when we were on the road and the village Ford was approaching. Not much to do for a dog, but then, you see, I loved him, in spite of his early coldness, and perhaps a little of my love found an answering note in his queer heart.

Let us get back to the garage, where we left Whoops giving us a rapturous welcome. During all this procedure, adorable whining noises are being produced, which rise to a crescendo as we alight. But only for a moment. For hardly has the first official formality been accomplished — (by which I refer to the hurried planting of two exceptionallymuddy paws on to the knees of my trousers), than he is off again, searching feverishly for a stone, or a stick, just outside the garage.

Now the object of this sudden search is *not* that I should play a game with him. Far from it. It has precisely the opposite function. It is a lure. A bait. The idea, you see, is that I should see this exquisite stone, and be so tempted by it that I should instantly try to possess it, and pursue Whoops out into the fields and the woods until I am far, far away from the hated car.

'He is not properly here yet', reasons Whoops. 'He has only just got out of that black shiny growling thing. He may get into it again. At all costs I must prevent *that!*' And so, when he has found the stone, he flaunts it before me, darting almost within reach and then pausing a few yards away. He tosses the stone in the air, catching it between his dazzling teeth, registering ecstasy. His eyes fix mine, his tail almost wags off, and all the time he is saying 'This is the *most* beautiful stone. *You* could not find a stone like this in the whole garden. It is a very precious stone indeed. I *might* let you have it, for a moment.' He comes a little nearer. The tail stops for one agonized moment, for I have turned to get a parcel from the car. But I shut the door again, and the tail starts anew. The stone is tossed in the air once more. I dart at it suddenly. Instantly Whoops is off, through the wood, a streak of animal happiness. I run after him, a streak of animal happiness too. And then I stop, breathless, and find I have run a hundred yards, and am in the middle of the field, with the blue sky above me, and buttercups at my feet. And I laugh out loud. For the week-end has begun.

CHAPTER XIV

WHOOPS CONTINUED

We will now give you a close-up of Whoops in his own home. This is a great privilege, allowed only to a few people.

We tiptoe out into the front garden, through an arch so thickly covered with purple clematis that it is as though the hedges were running wine. Up a tiny passage where, in spring, the white lilacs hang their pale heads in the shadow. Out onto a broad brick terrace in front of the kitchen. And here, on the terrace, is Whoops's house. He is not at home at the moment — having an illegal appointment with a rabbit — so we can examine his quarters undisturbed.

The kennel is very large, and stands at the foot of a big water-butt. It is also very beautiful, painted grass green, with a small flag stuck in the roof, and clean straw on the floor. It has a little drain running under its eaves to catch the rain, from the roof. This rain runs through a pipe the size of a pencil into Whoops's own particular water-butt, which is an old treacle tin, painted black.

At first there was a great argument as to whether Whoops should sleep in the kennel or indoors. I did not like the idea of putting a dog on a chain, and I thought that he might be cold. On the other hand, in a lonely country cottage you have to have a watch-dog, and if Whoops were always in front of the kitchen fire he would be of little value if anybody tried to break in on the other side of the house.

It was Whoops himself who decided it. He suddenly took a tremendous fancy to his kennel. He used to retire to it, on hot days, for purposes of meditation. He also used it to indicate that something had offended him. It was very easy to tell whether he was in retreat or merely sulking. If he was in retreat, he placed the tip of his nose outside the door, resting his face on his paws and casting his eyes up to the heavens, as though to say 'I am meditating, and should be glad to be left alone.' If offended, he went straight in and lay down without turning round, leaving a dejected tail protruding through the little door, like a black flag. However, it usually needed only a very few tactful words to set the flag flying again.

My favourite mental picture of Whoops is in this kennel. It is a cold winter's morning, and the ground is covered with snow. The snow lies thick on the kennel roof, making the red, white, and blue of the tin flag all the more brilliant. The snow lies thick on the water-butt, too, and on the ground outside. It is all white and glistening. Then slowly through the doorway comes a black woolly face, with two huge brown eyes. The face stays there for some time, a black blob against the universal white. And then the face sneezes and emerges, followed by the body. There is a yawn, a stretching, and a tremendous shake, which sends the snow flying like feathers from a bolster with a loose seam. Sleep is banished now, and Whoops is off into the garden, leaving wide-spaced prints of his paws over the sheeted lawn. In a few minutes those paws will be loaded with snow till they are as large as snowballs, and he will be coming to me to ask me if I will kindly comb them out as quickly as possible. In the meantime I have that beautiful picture to dwell upon — the black face coming gravely out of the kennel door . . . the yawn . . . the glimpse of a pink throat and dazzling teeth . . . and the warm, doggy breath drifting up, like steam, into the icy air.

Whoops is in his kennel every night at ten and off it every morning at six. During these night hours he is on the chain. I fought against the infliction of the chain for some time, but in the lambing season we were sternly warned by the neighbouring farmers that unless we kept him on a chain, he would be shot, and so we had no alternative. And now, he seems actually to like it. At any rate, when one says good night to him, he refuses to go into his kennel unless the chain has been fastened to his collar. I think he regards it as his badge of office, because, as soon as it is fastened on he sniffs it, shakes himself violently so that it clatters on the brick pavement, and then stalks into the kennel very solemnly, like a mayor who is about to declare the baths open to the public.

§ 11

It seems strange that there should be so much to tell you about Whoops, because really, apart from his appearance, there is nothing very remarkable about him.

He does no tricks, for example. To be quite frank I hate the idea of dogs doing tricks. I always feel embarrassed when I see spaniels pretending to be 'dead', or terriers catching pieces of sugar on their noses. The owners of these dogs may have taught kindly — may even be the best masters in the world — but I think that a dog standing on his hind legs is as undignified as a human being on all fours. You know, it isn't a bad plan, when you wonder how you ought to treat animals, just to forget that they are animals, and put yourself in their place. I know that I should very much resent having to fall on the floor and crawl over the carpet whenever I was offered a cocktail. And so I don't see why I should make my dog stand up for a piece of sugar.

He *can* beg . . . it is true . . . very unsteadily and uncertainly . . . with a broad grin on his face, to show that he does not really mind . . . but he very seldom does it when I am there. Because when anybody is holding up a piece of sugar for him, and tantalizing him to sit upright, I always seize a larger lump and pop it straight into his mouth, to the great indignation of my friends, who say he will *never* learn to beg if he is so spoilt . . . which is my nasty little intention.

I do not want him to 'perform.' I only want him to be his huge woolly self.

Consider, for example, the question of rabbits. Whoops never catches a rabbit by any chance whatever. But he has the most delirious fun with them. At the bottom of my garden there is a field with a hedge which is simply alive with rabbits. On warm summer evenings the rabbits sit up nibbling in the sun, looking very like those nursemaids who chew nougat with such grim determination along all our Southern promenades. As soon as we climb the hedge Whoops is off like a whirlwind. But he does not rush immediately at any particular nursemaid — I mean rabbit — no, he dashes down the whole length of the field, uttering piercing barks of delight, as though to warn the rabbits that closing-time has arrived. By the time that he has reached the end of the field not a rabbit is in sight. And then Whoops, assuming a very fierce expression, really gets down to business. He flies to rabbit-hole after rabbit-hole, sticks his nose inside, sneezes violently, sticks his whole head in, and then begins a tremendous scraping which sends the earth flying out behind him. He never scrapes very long at the same hole . . . there are too many other rabbity syrens, lolling in their subterranean caves, for him to be able to concentrate very long.

I often try to imagine the conversation the rabbits must have with each other during these proceedings:

Mr. Rabbit: There's that frantic bore again . . . when *will* he realize he isn't wanted? Why don't you complain . . . or write to somebody about it?

Mrs. Rabbit: What's the use? It isn't as if he did any harm. As a matter of fact, that doorstep *wanted* polishing.

Master Rabbit: Can't I go and make faces at him, daddy?

Mr. Rabbit: Certainly not! The idea!

Mrs. Rabbit: What's more, you won't go out of the back door until he's got as far as Number 10 . . .

Not very good . . . rabbits talk better than that, I expect. But it reminds me of something I wanted to say, i.e. that when the small 'master' rabbits are hopping about in the spring sunshine, Whoops is *not* taken to call on them. There was once an awful occasion when he nearly caught a tiny rabbit . . . it crouched in a furrow, screaming . . . . paralysed with fear. I shall never forget that scream. It made me feel sick.

We did not go rabbiting again till all the rabbits were grown up. And even now, if I think that Whoops is scaring them too much, I call him to heel. But this happens very seldom. The rabbits seem to have got quite used to Whoops. In fact, I believe they would really miss the occasional excitement he brings into their lives.

§ I I I

Whoops was not always called Whoops. His first name was Ogpu.

Ogpu, as it seems hardly necessary to say, is the name of the Bolshevik secret police. It always struck me as a rather comic institution, until a recent trial proved it to be a sinister one.

At first the name fitted Whoops perfectly. He looked like a Bolshevik, for one thing. His chief claim, however, to Ogpu membership was his inveterate habit of spying. You could not go into the garden for a single minute without seeing a black head peering from behind a bush, trying to find out if you were going a walk. If you went up to your room to fetch a book, the black head peered round the door. If you even rose from your desk, opened the window, and sniffed the morning air, the black head appeared from somewhere or other — even if you thought Whoops to be miles away.

Now this is really rather trying. It has such a con-stricting effect upon one's activities. For if, every time you look out of the window, or make a sudden move, you are immediately thought, by the spy, to be going for a walk, you become self-conscious about it. You try to act . . . you walk with a heavy step . . . you put a 'non-walk' expression on your face . . . because it is so dreadful to have to disappoint Whoops. You wish he would not always leap to conclusions, like this.

But he does leap to conclusions, on certain occasions. For example, when one is putting on one's boots.

Now there *are* occasions in life when a man may put on his boots without intending to go for a walk. He may have been working in his study, and put down his pen, in order to take a turn in the garden for ten minutes to refresh himself. But the paths are wet, and he is wearing slippers, so that he goes to the lobby to fetch his boots.

However, what is a man to do if he has a dog like Whoops, who, by some apparently ineradicable misconception, associates the putting on of boots as a definite declaration in favour of a walk? It is really an extremely exhausting problem. For this is what happens — (it happened only ten minutes ago, for the thousandth time):

I lay down my pen. I decide to go and see if the tobacco plant seeds have come up. I go to the lobby, fetch my shoes, and sit down on the sofa to put them on. But before I have laced up the first shoe, Whoops has discovered that I have left my desk, and is stretching himself before me.

'I observe,' he says, 'that you are putting on your shoes. You are therefore about to take a walk. And it is about time, too.'

To illustrate this remark he stretches, first with the front feet, then with the back.

'I shall be extremely pleased', he continues, 'to have an opportunity of leaving the extremely dreary quarters where I have been lying all the morning. There is very little of interest to be observed from under the dining-room table.' More stretching, and a loud and alarming sneeze. 'Still,' he resumes, 'we need not go into that. I see that you have at last got some sense into your head. You are putting on your shoes. You are therefore going for a walk. That is all that matters.' Another sneeze, and a violent shake, which begins at the head, and ends at the tail, or rather, at the whole hind-quarters, which vibrate violently long after the top part has finished shaking.

Now all this sounds as if it took a long time. Actually, it takes less than a minute. And it is a very trying minute for me. Because I have now to tell him that we are not going for a walk at all. 'No, Whoops. No. *Not* a walk. Not till after lunch.' And I pull down the corners of my mouth, and shake my head, and my voice vibrates with gloom.

The result is instantaneous, and desolating. The tail stops wagging and falls to half-mast. A hurt look comes into his eyes. I pat him, feeling like a criminal, but only manage to effect a slight twitch of that dreary tail, which, a moment ago, was so vibrant and so arched. And as I go out into the garden, I turn and see him standing in the doorway, very still, watching, and half the pleasure of the garden is spoilt.

Journeys to the post office are the worst of all. For when you go to the post office you really look as if you *were* going for a walk. I mean, you do go out of the front door, and down the road, and turn the corner, as though you were going, not to the post office, but to the green woods on the hill beyond.

However, how is one to explain all this to Whoops, whose paws are already scraping on the front door which I am about to open? I *do* explain it, of course. I lean over him, and say 'Listen, Whoops. We are only going to the post office. I have to send a telegram. While I am sending the telegram you will have to sit outside, or the post office dog will suddenly dart at you and teach you bad language and possibly bite holes in your nice woolly ears. You will have to sit by the little gate, and it will be boring for you. So really don't please get so excited.'

But it has no effect. He only wags his tail the faster. When I open the door he is half-way down the road before I shut it again. I call him back. He comes with many scamperings and liftings of front feet, making the sort of movements that I always think unicorns must make. All the way to the post office — about two hundred yards — these pranks continue. When we reach it, he trots past it, sniffing disdainfully. But somehow he has guessed that I am going in. For just beyond the post office he pauses, and looks back. First to me, and then to the green hills beyond. More than once I have failed to send an important telegram because I could not resist the pleading of those uplifted eyes.

§ I V

Whoops has never been beaten. Never, that is to say, since he belonged to me, and never, I believe, before.

Once I gave him one sharp slap, but the emotional result was so overwhelmingly out of proportion with any pain I could possibly have inflicted that I never tried it again. A verbal scolding is the worst he ever gets, and even that seems to affect him unduly. In fact, a frown is about all I dare go to.

This is apt to be a little tiring. For there are times, especially when a man is alone, and worried, when he cannot always be smiling. And it has practically come to this that I have to keep up a bright appearance for the sake of my dog.

What can you do, if two brown eyes are always staring at you, whenever you come out of your study? A chapter may be going wrong. You may have a headache. You may just have one of those unaccountable moods when you feel like plunging your hands in your pockets, kicking the furniture, and saying 'Hell,' and other even acider words. But if you go on like that in front of Whoops you will suddenly see a dejected black form creeping away behind the lilac bush. He has taken all your remarks personally. You may not even have known that he was there. (He always *is* there, but sometimes one forgets it!) But he saw you frown, and mutter beneath your breath, and kick a stone out of the way, and he thought it was all for *him*. And his sky darkened, and he slunk away.

What is one to do? Do *you* have to act like this, in front of your dog? To force a smile, and brace your shoulders, and look pleased, just because an indescribable bundle of wools and smells, with two brown eyes shining from it, is staring up at you? Heaven knows, I have never made such valiant efforts at cheerfulness with any woman as I have made with my dog. And only too often, these efforts fail. He knows I am acting, catches my mood, and slinks about, looking like a mute at a funeral — a funeral of which the undertaker has absconded, while he himself is suffering from the same complaint as the deceased.

§ v

Needless to say, he invariably chooses to give these performances on the days when Mrs. M. is visiting me.

No sooner does her footfall sound in the garden than Whoops, whom I have not seen all the afternoon, makes a sudden and miraculous appearance from behind a bush, wearing an expression of utter woe. His tail is down, the whites of his eyes are showing, and he creeps towards me as though under sentence of death.

Mrs. M. fixes a gimlet eye on him. 'Dear me' she says, 'your dog *does* look unhappy. Is he ill?'

'Not that I know of.'

'In disgrace, perhaps?'

'Oh no!'

'Perhaps somebody has been beating him?' Before the word 'somebody' she draws in her breath sharply, projects her rabbit's teeth, and looks at me as though my one pleasure in life were beating dogs.

'I don't think so, Mrs. M.' I reply, icily.

'One should *never* beat dogs,' says Mrs. M.

'I don't.'

'It is a great mistake,' she continues.

'I'm sure it must be.'

'It destroys their morale.' (She pronounces this *mawrahl*, with great relish.) 'Now my Cuckoo . . .'

'Your what?'

'My Cuckoo . . . surely you remember? When she was a puppy she was always pushing the other puppies out of the basket — so my husband called her Cuckoo. It was almost the last thing he ever did — so, of course, the name means *more* to me. My Cuckoo has never had a harsh word. Never.'

This, gentle reader, is a lie. It is really a terrible lie. Because Cuckoo has, in my presence, had a great many harsh words said to her, which, God knows, she deserved, being the most sleek, bulgy, disagreeable, slobbery dog that ever trailed the county. And apart from that, Mrs. M.'s sentimentality about the name is entirely false, because, for ten years before his death, Mr. M. was in a mental home, under the polite but firm impression that he was Napoleon.

And so, even if he did say 'Cuckoo,' he probably said it to his nurse, who certainly never found herself in a basketful of puppies, pushing them out.

§ VI

But do not let us end this chapter with Cuckoo. Let us go back to Whoops . . . and catch him in his happiest moment . . . just as we are starting for a walk on a June morning. We have our sticks in our hands, our cigarettes in our pockets . . . matches? Yes . . . but you'd better run back for a cap, because the sun's hot. That's better. All right . . . we can latch the gate, and away.

The hill stretches ahead of us. The hedges are starred, spattered, enamelled — any word you like — with wild roses — for the roses need many words for their many ways — words that light on the page as delicately as they swing on their branches — words that flush and pale and flush again, as the roses glimmer from white to deepest pink.

And so through high hedges, with roses above, and Whoops threading his ecstatic way through the thorns. These are the best moments that life has given me, and I say 'Thank you' for them, bowing low to the roses, and giving Whoops a cheerful pat as he flies past.

CHAPTER XV

EGGS AND HONEY

WHOOPS was such a success that during the third spring at the cottage I decided to have some more animals. The obvious animals to get seemed to be hens. But it was some time before I realized that if you want hens in the country, all you have to do is order them. You do not have to have a licence, nor pass an exam., in order to have hens. Nor do you need to run up an overdraft at the bank, nor build peculiar sheds for them, nor study their habits over much. Nor need you be under any fear that once they have arrived they will attack you, or develop frightful complaints.

But subconsciously, all these fears beset me when I first thought of having hens. I suppose it was partly due to the restrictions of childhood — for in my boyhood we only ran to cats — and partly to a habit of thinking in terms of the town. You cannot say to your valet, 'I think the flat needs some hens.' But you *can* say that to your gardener, and he will get some hens for you.

'How many hens will you be wanting, sir?'

'I think two would be enough, if they are fairly large hens.'

'Will you be wanting a rooster too?'

'Of course,' I said a little impatiently. 'Otherwise we shan't have any eggs.'

'You don't need a rooster, not for eggs, sir.'

I stared at my gardener. Was it necessary for me to
deliver to him, in sweet and homely language, a little
lecture on the Facts of Life? Was it possible that he had
reached the age of thirty-eight, and served in the Great
War, without realizing that he had not been born under
a gooseberry bush, that no stork had been in anyway
concerned with his arrival? And that obviously, if one
was going to have eggs, a rooster must be . . . to put
it mildly . . . in evidence?

'But S.,' I said . . . . 'I don't think you understand.
I want *eggs*. Hens don't just lay eggs like that.' ('Like
what?' I heard myself asking.) 'I mean . . . they don't
do it by themselves.'

'Yes they do, sir.'

'*What?*'

S. explained. It was some time before I realized what
he was telling me. That roosters are only required in
order to make the eggs produce chickens. That otherwise the hens can peck a bland and innocent path
through life without ever having heard of a rooster, and
yet produce eggs with the utmost regularity. I should
have thought that it must be a most ghastly strain on
their nerves. But there it is. Those were the facts. I
apologized to S. for having been so foolish, and went out
for a walk.

§ 11

In the lane I met Undine Wilkins, flouncing along
with a huge shallow basket under her arm, swinging a
sun-bonnet. Usually I avoid Miss Wilkins, but I was so
excited about my hens that I swung into step with her.

'I have just got two hens,' I said.

'*No!*' She gave the sun-bonnet an extra twirl. 'How delicious! What are they called?'

'Leghorns, I think. Everybody says Leghorns are the best hens.'

Undine pouted . . . . 'No . . . their own names. What are you going to call them?'

I told Undine that I had not thought as far ahead as that.

'Oh, but you *must!* What colour are they going to be?'

'White.' (I made a mental note to remember to tell S. that they must be white.)

'Then what about Faith and Hope?'

'It sounds rather pessimistic. As though they weren't going to lay any eggs.'

'Yes, perhaps it does.' She pursed her lips. 'The Dolly Sisters?' she ventured.

'I'm getting *hens*. Not peacocks. I mean pea-hens,' I added hastily, because I still felt a little confused by these mysteries of sex.

'Mary and Martha,' she observed, slightly damped.

'I don't want a Mary. I want two Marthas. And if they were both called Martha, the whole thing would lose its point.'

'It's terribly difficult,' she sighed. Then she suddenly brightened, and achieved a skip. 'Never mind! Let's find a name for the rooster! He'll be easy enough. Let's call him Peter. I adore Peters. *Do* call him Peter! Won't you?' She leant towards me, placing two fingers on my arm, her eyes pleading.

I looked Undine straight in the eyes.

'I'm not having a rooster,' I observed, in a voice that may, without conceit, be described as sepulchral.

'Not having a *rooster?*' Undine's face was a picture of dismay. 'Why not?'

I gloated over my superior knowledge. 'Why should I?'

'But your eggs? Don't you want eggs?'

'Certainly. I hope the Dolly Sisters, or whatever we call them, never stop laying eggs.'

'Then . . . .'

'Then what?'

Undine averted her eyes. She was evidently in the same state of primeval innocence as I had been a few minutes ago. We were strolling under an immense avenue of elms. The shadows were chequered at our feet. From the abundant meadows drifted a thousand sweetnesses, of young life throbbing through the earth to the exultant sun.

This, I am sure, she felt was a delicious situation. Like D. H. Lawrence. At any moment a peculiarly depraved gamekeeper ought to emerge from behind a blasted oak with a slain rabbit over his arm, and give her a look, and then where should we all be? At the end of the chapter, in a prickly bush of asterisks, I suspect, if it is an English edition.

What would have happened at that moment, I don't know, if Mrs. M. had not suddenly turned the corner. For in sixty seconds she had greeted us, told us that her cook had indigestion, scorned the remedies we suggested, discovered that I had ordered two hens, prophesied that they would eat up the garden and would remain perpetually sterile, and then, with a final jerk of her rabbit's teeth, shattered Undine's innocence in one graphic sentence which laid bare the strange self-sufficiency of hens, and the painful superfluity of roosters, in the matter of eggs.

Undine, bless her heart, turned bright pink at these revelations. I remember her, to this day, a pink face, under a sun-bonnet, in the shadow of the elms, with the ghostly Dolly Sisters chuckling behind her.

§ I I I

We did not call them the Dolly Sisters.

We called them Faint but Pursuing.

The accent was always put on the *But*. For when the hens arrived, they were a sad disappointment. I had fenced off a huge piece of the orchard for them, about the size of a tennis court, and had caused to be erected a substantial palace, with a front door, and three perches, and a floor of beautiful clean straw.

I also got a bucket of water, sank it into the earth, and arranged a delicate border of moss round it, so that the hens would think it was a pond. The hens, however, averted their eyes from it in horror, as though it were a well of poison. Why they did not die of thirst I cannot imagine.

However, to return to the names. The one which we called 'Faint' was very large and floppy, and of a dazzling whiteness. I am sure there must have been something the matter with it, because it was always wandering about with a vague expression, occasionally snipping off the head of a dandelion, assuming an expression of pained distaste, and dropping the dandelion from its mouth.

The other hen, 'Pursuing,' was very fussy, and was always bounding about after Faint. One was reminded of two ladies who had enjoyed a romantic friendship in their early youth, and the friendship had somehow gone sour on them, so that their energies were diverted into other channels. Faint, obviously, was a vegetarian, and Pursuing was interested in callisthenics. Faint would try to get off on her own. She would wander to one end of the orchard to find a dandelion. *But* . . . Pursuing would come bounding after her.

The hens stayed with me only three weeks. They were an unspeakable bore. For after one had watched them two or three times, there was nothing else to them. I tried to catch them laying an egg, but gave it up.

Besides, the eggs they laid were really as boring as they were themselves. Nobody will believe it, but I swear they laid stale eggs. The first time I found an egg it was very thrilling. Like finding a nugget. I went up to Faint and thanked her for it, but she only looked at me with weary disgust and disgorged a piece of half-chewed dandelion from her unpleasing beak. But when I found that all the eggs had thick bands of white on one side, and very thin bands on the other, like eggs that have lain in the grocers' for three weeks, I was less pleased.

Eventually, I decided that I had found out all there was to know about hens. So Faint but Pursuing were sold, at a charity fête.

I still think a rooster would have been a help.

§ I V

And now, in the air I seem to hear the strange and wildly disturbing sound of a thousand little wings. As though the orchestra were tuning up — as though the bows were feathering their way over the strings, and the flutes were giving tiny hysterical laughs — ('don't touch me, don't touch me, I'm ticklish,' the flutes always seem to say, before the curtain goes up) — and the 'cellos and basses are buzzing, glumly, foretelling doom to all of us, while the sweet breezes of the wood wind blow through the whole queer, disordered forest of melody.

For the bees are coming.

It was Maeterlinck who forced me to keep bees. Until this third year at the cottage I had never read his *Life of the Bee*. One goes through life, like that, leaving books unread, music unheard, pictures unseen, and though it is very reprehensible, in some ways it is comforting to think that there are so many lovely things yet to be learned.

I had not read more than fifty pages of this book, which is honeycombed with beauty, before I decided that if I did not get some bees at once life would be blank and empty for me. The particular passage of Maeterlinck which compelled this decision was one in which he describes the preparations the hive is making for the swarm. In unforgettable words he evokes 'the spirit of the hive,' which causes the bees to abandon their city at the moment when it is most prosperous and stored with wealth, to set out to encounter the hardships and perils of a distant country.

EGGS AND HONEY

'Never,' writes Maeterlinck,[1] 'is the hive more beautiful than on the eve of its heroic renouncement, in its unrivalled hour of fullest abundance and joy; serene, for all its apparent excitement and feverishness. Let us endeavour to picture it to ourselves — not as it appears to the bees, for we cannot tell in what magical formidable fashion things may be reflected in the 7,000 facets of their lateral eyes, and the triple cyclopean eye on their brow — but as it would seem to us, were we of their stature. From the height of a dome more colossal than that of St. Peter's at Rome, waxen walls descend to the ground, balanced in the void and the darkness; gigantic and manifold, vertical and parallel geometric constructions, to which, for relative precision, audacity and vastness, no human structure is comparable Each of these walls, whose substance still is immaculate and fragrant of virginal, silvery freshness, contains thousands of cells stored with provisions sufficient to feed the whole people for several weeks. Here, lodged in transparent cells, are the pollens, love-ferment of every flower of spring, making brilliant splashes of red and yellow, of black and mauve. Close by, sealed with a seal to be broken only in days of supreme distress, the honey of April is stored, most limpid and perfumed of all, in twenty thousand reservoirs that form a long and magnificent embroidery of gold, whose borders hang stiff and rigid. Still lower the honey of May matures, in great open vats by whose side watchful cohorts maintain an incessant current of air. In the centre, and far from the light whose diamond rays steal in through the only opening, in the warmest

[1] *The Life of the Bee,* by Maurice Maeterlinck. Translated by Alfred Sutro. George Allen and Unwin, Ltd.

part of the hive, there stands the abode of the future; here does it sleep, and wake. For this is the royal domain of the brood-cells, set apart for the queen and her acolytes; about 10,000 cells wherein the eggs repose, 15 or 16,000 chambers tenanted by larvæ, 40,000 dwellings inhabited by white nymphs to whom thousands of nurses minister.[1] And finally, in the holy of holies, of these parts, are the three, four, six, or twelve sealed palaces, vast in size compared with the others, where the adolescent princesses lie who await their hour; wrapped in a kind of shroud, all of them motionless and pale, and fed in the darkness.'

The thought of those princesses, lying in their pale shrouds, sipping sweetness in the dark, enraptured me. I put down the book. I would go out and get some bees at once. I glanced at the calendar. It said:

MAY 26

And then, it whispered, H.M. The Queen's Birthday.

I wished Her Majesty many happy returns and made a note to send her some honey next year. But as I did so, a little rhyme echoed through my head — a rhyme as ancient as many of the round, straw hives which are dotted about the villagers' gardens in Huntingdonshire:—

A swarm in May
Is worth a load of hay;
A swarm in June
Is worth a silver spoon;
A swarm in July
Is worth a fly.

[1]The figures given here are scrupulously exact. They are those of a well-filled hive in prosperity.

Already it was nearly June, and judging from the leisurely manner in which the average countryman worked, I would have to hurry if I was going to get a swarm that would even be worth a silver spoon.

So I ran out to the garage, leapt into the car, and sped down the lane to the next village, in search of Mr. Penthrift. For Mr. Penthrift, in the spare time that he can snatch from thatching, is a bee-keeper. And a very good one, too.

§ v

Mr. Penthrift was in the garden looking more like the Duke of Wellington than ever. I explained my business and asked him if he could let me have a swarm.

'It's getting late,' said Mr. Penthrift.

'But not too late? Can't you get a swarm at once?'

'Bees is funny things,' said Mr. Penthrift.

How funny they were, I did not even vaguely guess, at that time. However, he promised to do his best.

We went out to choose a hive. Now, I wanted a glass hive, so that I could watch the bees at work. But Mr. Penthrift said it would take him a long time to make a glass hive, and when anybody says that it will take a long time to do anything, in Huntingdonshire, you may be quite sure that he is telling the truth. So I contented myself with a pretty little white wooden hive, with a thatched roof. It was beautifully thatched in reed, and Mr. Penthrift said it would keep the bees nice and warm.

The more he talked about them, the more I began to understand why people who keep bees love them, in spite of the stings which they occasionally administer.

I began to walk up to one hive. Mr. Penthrift drew me back :—

'Never do that, sir. Never walk in front of the hive.' He shook his head. 'The bees don't like it. They might have to sting you.'

His concern was quite evidently for the bees, rather than for me. He did not want them worried. So we walked round at the back, and watched them coming and going. It was growing late in the afternoon, and there was a faint diminution in the tempo of their flight. They emerged from their tiny doorway, paused a moment, as though uncertain of their whereabouts, or dazzled by the sunlight, and then they sped away in widening circles.

I stayed watching the bees till the light was dim. Mr. Penthrift had long left me. I heard him in the kitchen, making beef-tea for his rheumatism.

When I went out I wanted to tell him that beef-tea was the last thing to take for rheumatism, and that if he really wished to be cured, he should live like the bees live, on honey and green things.

But one could not tell the Duke of Wellington to eschew beef-tea. It would savour of treason.

§ V I

The bees did not come till the end of June. For a whole month I had to wait, in an agony of suspense, while the flowers around me offered their sweets to alien bees. Whenever I went out into the garden and saw the bees drinking deep at the crimson heart of the roses, I felt like shooing them away, and saying, 'That rose is being kept for *my* bees.' But one could not shoo away a whole garden of bees. Besides, I began to like all bees, just because they were bees.

On the day that Mr. Penthrift brought them the calendar marked

JUNE 23RD

And then added, in the inevitable *sotto voce* —

H.R.H. The Prince of Wales's Birthday.

I was so delighted that as I ran out to greet Mr. Penthrift, who was standing in the lane, with the hive on a barrow, and all the bees shut up inside it, I vowed to send His Royal Highness two honeycombs next year. (Queen Mary, it may be remembered, was only going to get one.)

'Here we are,' said Mr. Penthrift. 'Where shall we put 'em?'

'In the orchard. Against the hedge.'

He wheeled in the hive. Gently he took it in his arms and deposited it on the grass. Then he took a long strip of wood from his pocket and placed it in front of the hive.

'What is that strip of wood?'

'That's their landing-stage. It's the thing they like to remember when they set off for their flights. You mustn't ever move it. Or they won't find their way back.'

I remember my Maeterlinck. I almost contradicted Mr. Penthrift. For Maeterlinck says — and I have proved him to be right:

'It is not the hive that they seem to remember, but its position, calculated to the minutest fraction, in its relation to neighbouring objects. And so marvellous is this appreciation, so mathematically certain, so profoundly inscribed in their memory, that if, after five months' hibernation in some obscure cellar, the hive, when replaced on the platform, should be set a little to right or to left of its former position, all the workers, on their return from the earliest flowers, will infallibly steer their direct and unwavering course to the precise spot that it filled the previous year; and only after some hesitation and groping will they discover the door, which stands not now where it once had stood. It is as though space had preciously preserved, the whole winter through, the indelible track of their flight: as though the print of their tiny, laborious footsteps still lay graven in the sky.'

However, this was too happy a moment for argument. I agreed with Mr. Penthrift that the landing-stage must not be moved the fraction of an inch.

'When shall we let the bees out?'

'I'd give 'em another hour to settle down.'

'And then I just pull this little slot in front of the hive.'

'That's right, sir.'

A few more injunctions, and then Mr. Penthrift went. I was alone with the bees.

I lay down on the grass and put my ear to the wooden hive.

Do you remember, when you were a child, putting your ear to a telegraph pole, and hearing, through the stolid wood, the high hum of the wind in the wires, or whatever it may be that causes that curious note that throbbed down into your young heart? Many is the hour I must have spent with my ear to telegraph poles, wondering if what I heard was only the wind, or if it was the mystic essence of a thousand messages, tragic, absurd, vital, or meaningless, that were speeding above me.

But that sound, strange and exciting as it may be, is as nothing to the sound of the bees in their hive.

Kneel down and listen. Come closer . . . they will not hurt you, for the shadows are falling, and the grass is already dewy . . . come closer, so that your ear touches the cool wood. Now, do you hear? The whisper of ten thousand wings? A whisper that never ceases, that hardly varies a semitone in its high, sweet note, and yet has in it an infinite variety of tone colours. If Mozart could have written an overture for the bees, and given them all magic flutes, made from blades of grass, this is the music he would have written. If Puck needed a choir for his wedding feast, here it is, singing eternally.

For here is the Song of Summer. If you listen long enough you will hear all the secrets the wind whispered as it wantoned through the hedgerows. You will understand why the leaves were fluttering, so madly, against your window at dawn, and why there was such a poignant sweetness in the scent of the bean fields.

You will hear all the things the flowers never dared to say.

You will hear all the things you never dared to say, yourself.

CHAPTER XVI

LEGEND

I FEEL too humble, when I think of the thousand secrets of the bees, to write very much about them. The few things I have discovered are so elementary that any experienced bee-keeper will smile at them.

The first discovery was a toad. A toad of quite paralysing ugliness, who seemed to come out of the bushes near the pond, just as the sun was setting, and crouched near the landing-board.

As first I thought that this monster might have a strain of poetry in him, and have come like a pilgrim, to listen in ecstasy to the evensong of the bees. But this pleasant illusion was soon dispelled. For, after I had watched him for a little while I saw his mouth open and snap over a poor, tired bee that had paused, for a moment, to rest on a dock-leaf before entering the hive.

This disgusting procedure was repeated several times. It was always the tired bees which he seized — the bees who had explored the furthest valleys and plundered most arduously the distant flowers. After seeing nearly a dozen bees devoured, I could bear it no longer. To pick up the toad myself was really a little too much to ask, so I asked the gardener to do it.

How many disagreeable things, when one comes to think of it, one asks the poor gardener to do! 'Oh S., there's a dead rat just by the farthest apple tree in the orchard. Do you think . . . ? Oh S., there's a most horrible smell in the tool-shed, as though, perhaps . . .

would it be possible . . . ? Oh S., there's a dead thrush in the greenhouse . . . would you mind?' I *do* try to clear things like this, as much as possible, but there are some things which I can't face. Dead animals, and live toads, are among them.

The next menace the bees had to face was a plague of wasps. Every time I went out to the hive there were a dozen powerfully built yellow wasps circling round the door, like enemy aeroplanes. Occasionally one would dart inside, and then there would be a battle royal. One bee, half the size of the wasp, tackled him by the throat, another stung him, and two or three watchers seized him by the legs, and after a tremendous tussle, threw him over the landing stage. However, I knew from Maeterlinck that one wasp could cause real havoc in a hive before he was ejected, and so I took the advice of an old bee-keeper and placed a stick of barley-sugar outside, on the landing stage. This stick attracted a dozen bees to the entrance, who fed with the utmost pleasure on it. There was therefore an additional body-guard always in readiness to drive the wasps away, as long as the barley-sugar lasted.

Of the manifold diversions the bees gave me, from the time of the first swarm till the time when I tasted the first spoonful of golden honey, I will not speak. I believe in doing things too soon, but not as soon as that! For the life of the bee is so unutterably mysterious that any man who knows a little about bees will agree with me that he knows nothing at all.

There is only one other thing I want to tell you about bees. I do not mind telling you this, because it is a legend.

§ 11

All poetry is a form of legend — it is a lesson
learnt, over and over again, through the dark and echoing centuries, by different men and repeated by them in
varying tones. And in the English country legends
(which thrive as thickly in our villages as the duck-weed
on the local pond) some of the loveliest legends of the
world are artlessly preserved.

It was my own housekeeper who told me the Legend
of the Bees. She has a way of throwing off remarks of
astonishing beauty as carelessly as a child throws away
the extra bluebell that will not fit into the bunch.
And quite casually, as though it were a perfectly ordinary thing to say, she observed one day:

'You know, if anybody should die in a house where
they keep bees, the master has to go to the door of the
hive, and knock, and tell them about the death, or
the bees will fly away.' And then, without any emotion,
she added 'Will you be dining at eight or half-past?'

Dining? At eight or half-past? I don't know. I don't
care. What does it matter how or when one dines after a
remark like that? For here is the very attar of poetry
— the last sad sweetness distilled — the ultimate chord
that poets seek — a chord undissolved, tremulous, struck
by searching fingers in the dark — a chord that will
never die away.

Oh to be a poet, when such a tale is told! Do you
remember Poe, and his *Rationale of Verse?* How he
beetled his brows, and ran his hands through his thick
black hair, and bent over his desk, working out *The
Raven* like a mathematical problem? What is Beauty?

he asked — and made a note in the margin. What is Music? he demanded — and made another note in the margin. What is the Most Poetical Thing? he cried — and went on with his notes. And then he added them all up, and wrote *The Raven*. A lovely poem, but an even lovelier piece of arithmetic.

But here, in this Legend of the Bees, is a subject that would have brought a flush to the thin cheeks of Shelley, and would have sent the blood coursing through Keats's veins like wine. Death . . . flowers . . . a message borne on wings . . . the sad drone of the bees . . . the sense of riotous, coloured life and pale, still death, with the blind flapping in the lazy breeze . . . what more could a poet ask than this?

§III

Till very late I sat in the dim light of my study while the bees seemed to drone around me. Yes — they ebbed and flowed around me, in tides of honeyed sound. I seemed even to see the glitter of their wings in the lamplight, like a film of trembling gauze. But through this gauze my eyes could not see. To the rhythm of their song I could weave no words, and from their sweetness I drew only the bitterness of frustration.

I wrote:

> Fly to the wild white cherry
> That makes the morning merry
> With dancing petals pale,
> And whisper her the tale

Of one who, ne'er again,
In sunshine or in rain
Will turn a shining face
Uplifted to your grace . . . . .

And then I drew an angry line through it. For *that* was a dancing lyric . . . its words were beribboned . . . there was a dreadful insouciance about it.

The bees droned on. I bent low over the desk and shut my eyes. I wrote:

Bear darkly down upon the purple vines
Cloud them with bitterness, suck dry their sweets,
Curdle a subtle poison in the wines
They carry in their veins . . . . .

But no. That was harsh and wry. I wanted music . . . I *had* music . . . but it would not flow through my pen.

It is a terrible thing to be filled with an emotion that one cannot express. People are always telling you, in these days, of the danger of suppressed sex. The dangers of suppressed poetry are surely greater.

For the room was charged, drunken, electric — any word you care for — with poetry. The white walls were thick with images. There were tall spires of lilies, up which the bees were slowly climbing, and ringing out their toll of death upon the silver stamens. There was a sense of flags being flown at half-mast — a thousand petalled flags which had suddenly shuddered in a bitter breeze, and fallen, fallen. As I looked at the white walls I saw them falling, as the bees hurried by with their dark message. Down fluttered the crimson of the rose and the white of the daisy — down dropped the purple of the clematis. And there was a sigh of desolation as the dewy jasmine leaned its sprays to the cold earth. And the earth itself was a carpet of dying blossom — a carpet that would be radiant for an hour, but was already shrivelling and blackening as the feet of death tramped over it.

Yet with all this tolling, this fainting, this sadness among the blossoms, with all this shadowy drift of beauty to the grave, I could make no poem. God — that is the ultimate bitterness — to put a pen in a man's hand, and then to freeze his hand, so that he cannot write.

Well, at least you will admit that I have been honest about it. And if the bees ever sing you a song — a true song — I would be glad if you would send it to me.

CHAPTER XVII

LUCIFER

As soon as I was able to break away from the enchantment of the bees, I went abroad for my annual brush and
polish in the South of France, and when I returned,
after nearly six weeks of absence, it was to find that
something of very great moment had occurred at
Allways. The electric light had arrived!

At least, that was how it seemed, as the car turned
from the Great North Road into the narrow lane that
leads, with such artless twists and caprices, to our
village. For here, stretching across the fields as far as
the eye could see, a line of gigantic pylons had suddenly
appeared. They must have been erected with incredible
speed, for they cut straight over meadow, stream and
coppice, and the last to be seen of them was in the far
distance, vanishing over the hill near the bluebell wood.

Now, there is a school of æsthetic thought which rules
that these pylons enhance the beauty of the landscape,
and in certain surroundings this may be true. For
instance, if one of them were erected in a public square
in Pittsburgh, it would be such an improvement on the
average building in that city that maidens would come
and nestle beneath it, in ecstasy, and little children
would look up at it with dewy eyes and lisp 'What is that
beautiful building, mummy?'

The members of the pro-pylon school have whole
dossiers of affectionate adjectives which they toss, like

flowers, around the feet of their steel monsters. They adore the 'gaunt significance' of the brutes. I do not. They may be suitable for an industrial landscape, or for the Sahara, with a foreground of niggers posed in peculiar attitudes, or for the backcloth of some very draughty little repertory theatre. But in the lazy fields of Huntingdon they seemed revolting.

I slowed down, and stared at them, trying to humanize them, trying to see in them a likeness to this or that, to blasted oaks, or skeletons, or strange soldiers. But the best one could tell oneself was that they were like a procession of acid and gigantic governesses returning from church, and that was not really very much comfort.

I pressed the accelerator, and sped down the lane. Once round the corner, came a sigh of relief. One could not see them from here. Round another corner, — another sigh of relief — they were still invisible. And so, all the way to Allways. As soon as the cottage was reached I dashed out into the garden. No, they were invisible. But wait . . . there was just one, far, away, over the tip of a tiny hill, like a particularly disgruntled governess who had been left behind. Well, it would be possible to bear that one. I christened her Ada Minks, blew her a kiss, and went in to lunch.

§ 11

It was soon very evident that the coming of the pylons had set the village in a pretty flutter of excitement. And it would be foolish to deny that I was as excited as anyone. Because obviously, now that the monsters were couched, so to speak, on our doorsteps, we should all be able to light ourselves from them. And though electric light is no great thrill in the town, it is a very great thrill in the country. I could not help thinking of all the amusing things an ingenious man might do with it, putting it high up in an elm tree, or in the bottom of a pond, or floodlighting the madonna lilies, till they looked far far lovelier than the Taj Mahal. Or he could place a single light burning in a rose-bush to amuse the moths, who would whirl mysteriously round it on still summer evenings. These airy visions, it must be admitted, were disturbed by the reflection that all these things sounded not unlike an ornamental tea-garden, but none the less, the visions persisted. They were still very vividly in my mind when I went out for the afternoon walk and met Mrs. M. hurrying across the village green.

'You've seen the pylons?' said Mrs. M. breathlessly.

It would have been quite impossible for any man to deny that he had seen the pylons. Besides, I really wanted to know what was going to happen. So I said 'yes' and asked Mrs. M. what it all meant, and would we have electric light at last, and if so, how and when.

To all of these questions Mrs. M., needless to say, had precise and accurate answers. In fact, there was hardly time to put the questions at all, so rapidly was she breathing and so urgently was she protruding her rabbit's teeth, in an agony of suppressed information.

'Yes' said Mrs. M., 'we can have it at once, if we get ten people.'

'Are you sure?'

'Perfectly sure. They have it already at Yaxley, and they only have nine there, one of whom is old Mrs.

Gable, who only uses it for an electric toaster, which I think is most extravagant.'

'Could *we* have electric toasters?'

'You could have electric hares if you wanted,' said Mrs. M., and she laughed very loudly, sharply, and authoritatively, and was quickly grave again. Mrs. M.'s laugh is like a Jack-in-the-box. It seems to spring at you from the sober casket of her body, startle you with its metallic rattle, and then, before you have time to laugh back, it snaps back again, and all is quiet and grave.

'Have you made inquiries as to who wants it?' I asked.

'Quite unofficially, I have. The vicar, of course, is most anxious. Then there are the C's and the H's. That's three. Then there's me and the post office . . . five . . . and you, naturally.'

'Yes. But that only makes six.'

'Then there's Miss Wilkins. . . .'

'But surely you know she's always said electric light in a Tudor cottage was "sacrilege"? She raves at the very thought of it. And anyway she's just laid in a vast stock of Tudor candles.'

'How do you know?'

'I saw the odd man stowing them away in her tool-shed.'

'In her tool-shed?' A gleam came into Mrs. M.'s eyes. 'In that case, the rats will eat them', she observed, with much relish. 'And she'll have to buy a new lot. And by the time she's supplied all the rats of the neighbourhood with enough Tudor candles to keep them going through the winter she may possibly realize that we're living in the twentieth century.'

'If she ever realized that, Mrs. M., she would pass away.'

At which Mrs. M. only projected her rabbit's teeth, and snorted.

Mrs. M., however, was not to be deterred by the obscurantist tendencies of Miss Wilkins. She had no doubt whatever that she would get ten people — 'I could get fifty if I really put myself to it,' she proclaimed, in her intoxication. 'There is the shop, for example.'

'Mrs. Joy doesn't look like the sort of woman who wants electric light.'

'Have you seen her lately? No? Then you may as well realize that you are making a great mistake. Mrs. Joy is a changed woman. She has put up a new notice. . .'

'*No?* What is it this time?'

Mrs. M. pursed her lips, and then intoned: '*Please examine your change before leaving as no mistakes can be rectified afterwards.*'

'She's put that up . . . in the shop?'

'Yes. In red ink.'

This was such a glorious piece of news that for the moment it quite obscured the distant vision of the electric light. For though Mrs. Joy was partial to placards in her shop, and though one might always be quite sure, when one went in to buy a box of matches or a roll of string, that some fresh injunction would be staring at one from the wall, relative to the undesirability of dogs in commercial establishments, or to the desirability of cash transactions, or, more generally, to the beneficial qualities of the human smile, the shortness of life, and the undoubted presence of the sun behind the clouds — somehow this last notice seemed the best of all.

'*Please examine your change before leaving as no mistakes,*'
etc. Mrs. Joy had evidently been up to London lately.
Puzzled and flustered she had edged her way into the
Underground, and while she was fumbling in her bag
for her sixpence her eye had caught that notice, and it
had seemed good to her, and she had put it away in her
nice old brain, which was as sweet and fresh and juicy
as an apple that has been stored, through the autumn
months, in a cool old barn; and when she got back
to Allways she took a piece of paper and bent over
it and very carefully, with many deep breaths, she wrote
that slogan. Then she held it before the fire, and the
light of the flames caressed it and dried the ink, and
then she shuffled out of the parlour, into the little shop,
and opened a new penny packet of drawing pins and
carefully, very carefully (because her hands were old
and her eyes were not so good, these days) she pinned
it up on the wall. And then she looked at it, many
times, turning her head this way and that, while the
light of the flames drifted through the parlour door
like dancing spirits, pricking golden points in her white
hair, gilding, for a brief, capricious instant, the network
of wrinkles about her throat, casting a momentary
beauty about the still poise of her clasped hands. . . .

'*Please examine your change before leaving, as no mistakes
can be rectified afterwards.*'

An incantation, that — a mystery, a strange fantastic
litany, to Mrs. Joy. And in very real humility, to me.
For there is a cargo of beauty, borne over the seas of
thought, in the emptiest sentences of mankind, if only
the winds of the spirit blow kindly. And how rich was
that cargo which Mrs. Joy had brought back to Allways,

in that little sentence, it needs a man with only the smallest grain of poetry in him to see. For does it not bring with it a vision of a door opening and closing, opening and closing . . . and a tiny bell that tinkles through the seasons . . . striking its sweet silver note against an accompaniment of so many moods of Nature's orchestra . . . ringing against the turgid swell of autumn winds . . . against the sob of the rains of spring . . . against the quiet, melodious hush of July mornings . . . against the icy quiet of winter? The bell tinkles, the young men enter, and fumble for their sixpences; the old women pass in, and put their shillings on the gnarled counter; the children peer up, their eyes sparkling for sweets, and part with their pennies. The door swings, the little procession passes, in and out; the picture, through the window, changes from grey to green, from green to red, from red to white. And always, Mrs. Joy stands there . . . .

'Please examine your change before . . . .'

'How many *more* times are you going to repeat that sentence?'

I blinked. There, in the sunlight, was the face of Mrs. M. It was a shock to see it so suddenly.

'Don't you see, now, why Mrs. Joy is obviously a woman who wants electric light?'

'Not entirely.'

'Well, the shop is always as dark as a cave. And if people are going to examine their change, they can't do it in the dark. It's impossible.' Mrs. M. shook her head violently, as though somebody were about to deny the truth of this assertion. 'I shall go and point that out to Mrs. Joy', she continued. 'I shall point it out to her

personally. I shall show her how *illogical* it is — to
say the least of it — to put up a notice about examining one's change and then to give one no opportunity
of doing it. I shall tell her that I don't see why I should
step out into a muddy road just to see if I have got
elevenpence or elevenpence halfpenny, when by
merely turning on a little switch the whole thing
becomes as clear as daylight.'

Those who know Mrs. M. will agree that she would
cheerfully wade through a bog in order to 'examine her
change.'

But the narrative is flagging. It may therefore be
recorded that Mrs. M. engaged herself, in the near
future, to make Mrs. Joy join the electric brigade. She
also persuaded me to come with her to Miss Wilkins,
on the following morning, in order to lay siege to that
young lady's obstinacy, to make her realize, as Mrs. M.
repeated, that 'she was living in the twentieth century.'

§ I I I

It was very clear indeed that La Belle Undine had
been expecting us, because such very elaborate preparations had been made to show that she was not!

When, on the following morning, we unlatched the
little gate that opens from the road into her cottage
garden, we were instantly greeted by the outburst, from
a back room, of Mimi's *Addio* from *Bohème*. It was as
though, by opening the gate, we had automatically
turned on a gramophone record. Unfortunately, however, it was not a gramophone which was making this
noise, but La Belle Undine herself. And the noise

continued all through the loud tattoo which Mrs. M. made on the door with her umbrella. (She scorned, for this purpose, the antique dolphin which Undine had caused to be hung up as a knocker.)

The singing ceased — (just before a phrase which contained a tactless G natural) — and there was silence. Then came the frolic of feet down the bare staircase, the door burst open, and Undine with a peal of astonished laughter cried:

'Oh my dears, I thought it was the milk!'

Anything less like milk than Mrs. M.'s face, at that moment, could not be imagined. For though she has her faults, Mrs. M. is an honest woman, with an almost fanatical hatred of affectation. And the idea of Undine thinking we were 'the milk' at eleven o'clock in the morning, was so galling to her that if she had not arrived to plead for favours, she might have made some very acid remarks. As it was she contented herself with a hoarse 'so amusing' and pushed her way inside. Undine followed us.

'So lovely of you to come in,' she crooned, taking Mrs. M.'s arm, 'If I'd only known.'

Mrs. M., detaching herself as gracefully as possible said 'We're not disturbing you?'

'No . . . no . . . I was just tidying up my box-room.' She held out her hands (which were coated with liquid powder and had nails polished as red as raspberries) . . . . 'You see . . . absolutely black!'

Mrs. M. regarded the hands, and said nothing.

'And this room . . . just a *litter!*'

I looked round at the 'litter.' True, there was a certain abandon, but it was so effective an abandon that it seemed difficult to believe that it could have been obtained entirely by chance. On the very top of a pile of illustrated magazines, for example, there was a copy of *The Sketch*, open at a picture of a lovely lady, bearing a very faint resemblance to Undine. The lady was standing against a cedar tree, which was the pride of Undine's garden, and underneath the picture was the caption:—

> The Hon. Undine Wilkins
> The Latest Recruit to the Rural
> Delights of a Cottage Garden

However there was no time to make a detailed examination of the 'litter,' because Mrs. M. advanced to the attack without further delay.

'I expect you know why we've come,' she remarked, sitting down heavily on a Knoll settee.

'No. I haven't the faintest idea', said Undine, with great innocence.

'Well — you've seen the pylons?'

'Pylons?' Undine's innocence increased. 'Pylons? What are they?'

Mrs. M. projected her rabbit's teeth. She spoke very crisply. 'They are to be seen in large quantities in all the fields near the Great North Road. If you have *not* seen them, it must have been a very dark night. If you *have*, I can assure you that they are not scarecrows, nor the foundations of cathedrals, but objects for the transmission of electric light.'

All this was said with great speed and ferocity, and it was to be concluded that Mrs. M. had opened a declaration of battle. This was enthralling to watch, but regrettable from the immediate object we had in view. So, very gently, I leant forward and said:

'We think that they may be bringing electric light to the village.'

Undine turned to me. She opened her eyes in astonishment. 'No?' she breathed. Then she nodded, 'Oh yes. I remember. I did hear something about it.' She switched back to Mrs. M. and shook her head, at the same time achieving a brave smile. 'Never mind,' she said. 'We'll hope it's only a rumour, won't we?'

Mrs. M. stood her ground. 'But it's a great deal more than a rumour,' she said.

Undine made a gesture which was intended to convey that the subject was really too painful to discuss. 'Yes?' she shrugged her shoulders. 'The Philistines we have always with us,' she observed. And then, as though dismissing the subject, she said 'Cigarette?'

She rose from the sofa, grasped a silver cigarette box and held it out to me. Her hand was shaking, and I realized that this was because she too was in full array of battle.

Mrs. M. now came out into the open.

'You mean, you dislike the idea of it?'

Undine turned round, vaguely. ' The idea of it? Oh — the electric light?' she laughed. 'Still that subject Oh, no, Mrs. M., I don't dislike it. . . .'

'Then why . . .'

'Dislike is *not* the word I should use,' said Undine, with a smile that can only be described as tigerish. 'Nor should I use the word "detest." Nor the word "hate." In fact, I don't really think I know any word that could convey what I feel — what I'm sure we *all* feel — about such an idea.' She was quivering with suppressed fury. Once again her hand gripped the cigarette box. I saw something flashing before me, and heard a deceitfully dulcet invitation to have a cigarette, but before there was even the chance to decline, the box was switched away from me, Undine was standing by the fireplace, and Mrs. M. had observed:

'Some of us are living in the twentieth century.'

'And some of us are living in the century we create.'

'I'm sure that's very clever, but it seems to me selfish. . . .'

'Oh, Mrs. M. . . .'

'To refuse the benefits of electric light to the rest of the village just because *you* think that Queen Anne is still on the throne.'

Undine's eyes were blazing. 'I am not refusing any-body anything,' she said. 'As far as I am concerned, you can all live in a perpetual blaze of electric light. If people wish to put dynamos in their drawing-rooms and have jazz in the church . . . .'

'There was no suggestion of jazz in the church . . . .'

'No? Then I expect that will come later.'

And then, for a moment, there was a frightful silence. Mrs. M. was sitting bolt upright on the Knoll settee drumming her fingers on her knees. Undine was tapping her foot very hard on the super-Tudor fire rail. Both ladies were darting swift and jerky smiles, in my direction, smiles that seemed to be forced out of them by some very painful inward spasm. It was obvious that some sort of intervention was necessary, so I said:

'I don't think we ought to quarrel about it, but . . .'

'Quarrel?' echoed Mrs. M.

'Quarrel?' laughed Undine. 'Are we quarrelling?'

'I was only going to say that as you are afraid that it may spoil the village, I was wondering if we couldn't put in some sort of safeguard, saying that the light must be for strictly domestic use, or something like that?'

Undine shook her head. 'My dear,' she said, 'it's sweet of you. And, of course, the idea of suggesting safeguards in *your* case is absurd, because *you* have taste . . . although even with *you* I regret it . . . those lovely old lamps. But it's *me* I'm thinking of.' She shuddered and put her hands over her eyes. 'Those dreadful wires running over these old beams. . . .'

'They could all be painted over . . . they could be quite invisible,' urged Mrs. M., almost politely.

'Not to me,' said Undine, '*I* should see them. And then my lamps . . . and candles fluttering in the wind . . . what was it Meredith said?'

This was too much for Mrs. M. 'How you can pretend to like candles in a draught, I don't begin to understand.'

'I never expected you to begin to understand, Mrs. M.'

It was evident that the brief truce was over. I tried to intervene again, but it was too late. Mrs. M.'s voice rose:

'Dripping ugly wax all over the brass.'

'I happen to think that wax on brass is extremely beautiful.'

'Perhaps you *may*,' snapped Mrs. M., 'but we haven't all of us got three maids who can spend a whole morning scraping wax off candlesticks.'

'Really? And *has* anybody in the village got three maids?'

'Nobody but you, my dear.'

'Now, that *is* interesting.' Undine put her finger to her forehead, as though engaged in deep thought. But she was really vibrant with triumph, because she had caught out Mrs. M. in a domestic inaccuracy, and she knew, and I knew, and Mrs. M. knew that we both knew, that nothing would more enrage her, the local encyclopædia, than the thought that she imagined there to be three maids when there were only two.

'*Most* interesting,' continued Undine, looking up with tremendous innocence. 'Because I thought I had only two. Dear me! A new maid must have popped in by mistake. . . .'

'Well, however many maids you may have . . .' began Mrs. M., with agony in her voice . . .

'But I have *three*, Mrs. M.,' said Undine, who was not going to allow this exquisite triumph to be so summarily dismissed. 'You've just told me so yourself, so it must be right. I only wish I knew what this third maid, whom I have never seen, was called, and what she looked like, and what wages I paid her. Perhaps you could tell me all those things, too, Mrs. M.?'

This was the end of Mrs. M. Baffled in her quest, and exposed in her ignorance, she decided to beat a voluntary retreat. And so she rose abruptly to her feet, held out her hand and said:

'Well, it seems that there is not much point in discussing it any further.'

Undine graciously took her hand. To me she said, 'Must you be going?'

'I'm afraid so.'

'*Do* come in one evening . . . if you can bear the sight of candles in the breeze?'

'I'd love to . . .'

But Mrs. M. was already in the hall, calling to me, and there was no time for the making of sentimental rendezvous, so I took my leave.

As we walked away from Undine's cottage, we heard once again the strains of her voice, singing *Bohème*. And this time she did not flinch from the phrase with G natural in it. In fact she attacked it with such zest that it sounded suspiciously like G sharp.

§ I V

'Detestable woman!' muttered Mrs. M. She was so angry that as she walked she kept digging her stick viciously into the hedge as though she had a grudge against the brambles. 'Detestable! I don't believe it, either.'

'Believe what, Mrs. M.?'

'She always had three maids. Old Mrs. Charles, Ada, and that French girl she brings up from London. Oh! Perhaps *that's* what she meant. If so, I call it a downright lie. What do you think?'

I did not at all follow the trend of Mrs. M.'s remarks, and told her so.

'I mean,' said Mrs. M. impatiently, 'that the French girl wasn't counted. Just because she happens to take her up and down from London. That *must* be it. And so I call it a downright lie. The French girl's a maid, isn't she?'

'I hope so, Mrs. M.'

Mrs. M. snorted, and walked on. She swung her stick very viciously at a lovely patch of cow-parsley with feathery cream-coloured blossoms. To my great relief she missed it. And so we returned to our respective homes.

However, before we parted, she gave signs that there was still a good deal of fight in her. She prophesied that Undine would bitterly regret the morning's work, and drew a gloomy picture of her, sitting in the dark, listening to the rats gnawing at the Tudor candles in the tool-shed. She then drew an alternative picture of ourselves, laughing and frolicking in a blaze of light, as though we were at the White City. In fact, she was so exalted by the pleasures that were in store for us that I began to wonder whether, after all, Undine had not been right in her forebodings, whether Allways might not lose, by this innovation, a good deal of its mystery and charm.

A Bedroom

CHAPTER XVIII

I OBEY ANTINOUS

BUT alas for our hopes! It was only a week later that they were all destroyed, as though by a sudden spit of flame from those very pylons which we had all been worshipping.

I was not in Allways at the time, but it appears that one afternoon a young man ('from the Government,' as he was afterwards described) drove up to the vicarage in a high-powered car ('for which *we* pay,' snorted Mrs. M.) and demanded to see the vicar. The vicar was in the garden, and as he hurried indoors, wiping the earth from his knees, his mind was full of hope — indeed, of praise; it was as though he already saw the light glittering merrily behind the dim blue windows of the church, illuminating the clouded panes till they shone like sapphires.

He found, in his study, a young man in a great hurry. He was in such a hurry that to this day the vicar cannot quite realize what happened. All he knows is that before he had a chance to speak, the young man had delivered a shattering indictment of Allways from the point of view of electrical interest, had said a great deal about wattages, voltages and such horrors, had deplored the ignorance of a community that imagined that it only had to connect a wire with the main current in order to obtain light, had thrown out the sarcastic suggestion that *if* there were a millionaire in the village who would like to pay £10,000 for a decentralizing plant, the matter might be considered, but otherwise he hoped that no more would be said about it, because people in government offices were very busy these days, and, thank you, he could find his own way out.

He was gone before the vicar could shake hands with him. The noise of the car vanished up the lane. The vicar sighed. Well, that was that. He walked slowly to the open door, through which one has a very pretty view of the church. As he stood there, the sun leapt from the clouds, like a bright sword unsheathed. A stream of light flashed on the church windows — light from above, light from God. The windows twinkled merrily, as though they were laughing at the vicar for worrying about them. He stood there, and gradually he began to smile, feeling that all was for the best in this world, as indeed it is, if one's mind is in tune with the simple realities of life, and not perpetually jangling with the discords of man.

§ 11

Such moral consolations, however, were denied to most of us. When the vicar told us what had happened, we could not believe it. The pylons were there — as plain as daylight — carrying wires with enough electricity to light the whole country — why could we not tap a little of it for our own use? Surely, if a great river is running at the bottom of your field you can cut a little stream from it? That was how it seemed, to our limited intelligences. We could not realize how powerful the current was.

'I've seen birds perching on 'em, at any rate,' said Mrs. Joy, who, contrary to all expectations, had leapt at the idea of electric light, in order that we might all examine our change like gentlemen. 'Yes,' she said, 'many a time I've seen birds perching on 'em. And if the electricity can't kill a couple of sparrows, I don't see that it can do much 'arm to us!'

Some of us had already sold our spare lamps, and others had promised them to the next jumble sale. Already the rural district council had discussed the possibility of having a 'rustic' light on the village green. And now we were all to be plunged into darkness again. It was a bitter disappointment.

Needless to say, the loudest in her protests was Mrs. M. She had completed her list of ten people. Indeed, she had made it up to eleven, if you can count Mrs. Joy's niece, who was a little weak in the head, and only wanted the electric light 'for her fowls' (a mysterious phrase, which the reader may interpret to his own satisfaction). It was therefore particularly galling to her that she had taken all this trouble for nothing.

'It is an outrage,' said Mrs. M. 'Putting those monstrous things almost in our back yards and then refusing to allow us to use them. I've a good mind to run a private wire up one of their wretched poles and tap it off myself.'

'If you did you'd electrocute the whole population of Huntingdon.'

'I sometimes think that some of them would be all the better for a little electrocution,' she snapped.

The only person who was really pleased was Undine. She was positively floodlit with satisfaction. She beamed more brilliantly than she had ever beamed before.

'So sad about your electric light,' she purred, when I met her in the lane. I muttered something about the electric light not being my idea, exclusively.

'Oh, no, of course. It was Mrs. M. . . . our great modernist! She *must* be disappointed about it.'

I offered no opinion on that point.

'I shall have to send her a box of candles, as a consolation prize!' And Undine, with many a purr and gurgle, tripped away from me, into the mists of the Tudors.

Had Undine carried out her threat, I hesitate to think what might have happened. However, she did not, for the simple reason that shortly afterwards, the Tudor candles, as Mrs. M. had prophesied, were all devoured by the rats. It was the one bright spot on an otherwise dark horizon.

Rats, as Mrs. M. said, will eat anything.

§ 1 1 1

And there, I suspect, the matter would have ended, had it not been for Antinous, and a snowstorm.

Antinous is the only statue in my garden. Even if I wanted more statues, I should never be able to have them, because Antinous is so beautiful that he would put all the other statues to shame. They would fold their grey marble arms over their faces, and drift away, to hide in the woods.

Antinous stands in the middle of a tiny lawn, receiving perpetual homage from a little circle of flowers that are always in bloom round his feet . . . a circle of flame that is never allowed to die down. It was from this lawn that he issued, quite unexpectedly, his commands about the electric light.

It happened like this. One night in the depths of winter, I arrived at the cottage alone. I had driven through a blinding storm of snow. My head was awhirl with the pattern of snowflakes dancing up to the windscreen, flecking the glass, melting. It had been a relief to turn up the little lane that led to Allways. Still more was it a relief, after I had warmed myself at the remains of a log fire, to step out into the dark garden, to feel the virgin snow beneath my feet, and to hear no sound . . . no sound at all . . . for the dark skies were too busy unloading their white sorrows to allow any wind to blow.

I pulled my coat round my chin and felt in my pocket for the little torch which I always carried. It threw a white rod of light in front of me. I hardly knew why I was wandering down the garden like this — the snow was too deep for me to make any discoveries — one would have to make many agonized scratchings before one could find even the hard points of the snowdrops. Yet I walked on and on until suddenly I realized that I was walking over the little lawn, where Antinous stood. Yes — here he was! But . . . But . . .

As though frozen, I stayed quite still.

For Antinous, in the light of the torch, was as an angel shining. The ivory skin was pranked with silver, and the snow drifted round his limbs like the petals of sad white roses. On his exquisite shoulders the snow had gathered as a mantle, and over his brow it glistened in diamonds.

I moved the torch, very gently. Ah — that was superb! A million diamonds sparkled, for an instant, against the deep tapestries of night, and now, the torch being still, he was poised again, in new proportions. The shadows had made a delicate shift. Under the chin they lay deeper, but from the young breast they had flown away . . .

Down, down drifted the snow, in sweet and icy measure. If you held your breath, you could hear the flakes whispering as they reached their journey's end . . . whisper after whisper, until the earth was enfolded in a strange and secret mantle. But always I held the light to Antinous, and always he regarded me with his pale marble eyes.

Was it joy or sorrow that I was to read in those silvered features? Had the mouth twisted to a smile, or was it a trick of the frost? Were those tears in his eyes, or only snowflakes dancing? I moved the torch again, trying to discover the secret. But always Antinous kept his secret. He sparkled, he shone, he paled in the shadow, as I moved the torch. But always he kept his secret — he remained a white and lovely enigma against the fathomless curtains of the night.

I went in. I sat by the fire. The flames seemed cheap and cold. Even the gayest sparks that the dying logs could offer, the rosiest glow that came from the heart of the burning ash — even those were tawdry and artificial. Shapeless. I hated them. I wanted Antinous only, shining before me, in icy elegance. God . . . there was beauty . . . the ultimate beauty, surely. A statue in the snow, lit by a torch. A fragment of marble, superbly carved, isolated, illuminated against the universal night. A piece of form, silhouetted against the grim formlessness of the dark . . . the dark . . .

I stared at the logs. They irritated me. I gave them a kick and went up to bed.

And that is why I have electric light in my cottage.

CHAPTER XIX

NIGHT'S CANDLES

Of the installation of the electric light, the arrival of the engine, the transformation of the little garage into a miniature power station, the fascinating rows of batteries which were ranged along the shelves, the first wild whirr of the engine, I dare not write. (As a matter of fact, the engine does not make a wild whirr, but a nice chuff-chuff, like a very large cat, ruminating after a meal.) However, I am a congenital idiot about mechanical things, and will merely state that it seems to me an ideal engine, because it never goes wrong, and does not make any smells, and only has to be turned on for a few hours every week. And it is quite hidden behind a pile of silver-birch logs in the garage.

Nor will I delay you with a description of Mrs. M.'s face when she heard that I was going to have an independent plant of my own. Nor of the intrigues she made (and still makes) in order to persuade me to let her have just *one* line from my plant in order that she might have electric light of her own.

'So simple, it would be,' she pleaded . . . 'just a line over that elm, and across Mrs. Joy's paddock.'

'But it would hang down, and catch in the loads of hay, Mrs. M.'

'No, it wouldn't. Or if it did we could run it underground.'

'The Parish Council would never agree to that.'

'If *I* spoke to them . . .'

'But, Mrs. M., I don't think there would be enough electric light for two.'

'Of course there would. Besides, think of the fee I should pay you!'

I *was* thinking of it. Mrs. M. I was certain, would hardly pay enough for the sign that I had planned to put over Whoop's kennel. It was to be a very gay little sign, with these words in tiny diamond letters:

Whoops Varieties Limited,
Rabbits Warmly Welcomed.

Mrs. M. continued: 'It isn't as if you were going to live in a perpetual blaze of electric light.'

'I *was* going to have an electric iron,' I ventured.

'Why? Why do you want an electric iron?'

I could think of no answer to this question, apart from the obvious one 'to iron things with,' which seemed, somehow, devoid of epigrammatical brilliance. So I took refuge in dark mysteries of wattages and voltages, knowing that Mrs. M. was as ignorant of these matters as I was.

After we had said 'What' at each other for a long time, and had become more and more irritated because we did not know whether we meant 'what' or 'watt,' the matter dropped.

Mrs. M. never got her electric light. I warn her that she never will. I had to work like a slave to pay for mine, so why should she have it, when she only has to sit back and draw an income from Indian four per cents and Southern Preference Railway and things like that? I ask you!

But though there is much that I cannot tell, there is a good deal that I positively insist upon telling, in order that you may share with me the thrill which the final arrangement of the lights gave me. I have a sneaking suspicion that you feel the whole thing was a mistake. That the cottage would have been nicer if we had kept to lamps.

You will not think so when you learn how we set about it. For I wanted the lights for their dramatic value, rather than for their convenience. And I believe I succeeded in getting what I wanted.

Here, then, is the list of lights, as finally settled and executed.

1. *Antinous*

I made it quite clear that if Antinous could not be lit, there should be no lights at all. The electric man, who came up from London, said that there would not be the least difficulty about lighting Antinous, and arranging for a switch that could be turned on from the Garden Room.

And so it was done, by a little wire, carefully hidden behind banks of May and lilac, sending its magic sparks in secret. Just before it reaches Antinous, it dives underground, threads its way through the roots of the roses, and emerges in a funny little glass box at Antinous's feet. This box is sunk level with the ground, and is always fringed with low-growing flowers, aubretias, lobelias, candytuft, and the like. In winter it is packed close with snowdrops, who stand round in a tiny square, like ballet girls waiting to dance.

Seven or eight books might be written on this light at
the feet of Antinous. It has given me more pleasure than
any theatre has given me, more strange surprise than the
vision of any distant coast at dawn. Night after night
one can wander round Antinous and always the shadows
seem to be dancing in a new rhythm. One of the loveliest
times to see him is in summer, when the nights are thick
and violet and velvety, and mysterious with moths. The
moths come from far and near, borne on wings that are
powdered with the dust of ancient jewels, and as they
come into the circle of light they flutter round, in a
drugged ecstasy, with many a faint spark of green and
gold, as the light caresses them. I stare and stare until
it seems that I, too, am a fluttering moth . . . drugged by
beauty . . . conscious that somewhere there is a strange
white fire which I cannot find . . . a lofty, luminous
figure round whose feet I vainly drift . . . searching,
fluttering, adoring . . . adoring, fluttering, searching . . .
Even laughter I have had, from this little light. For
after dinner, when susceptible people are staying at the
cottage, when the wind blows high and the shadows on
the ceiling are like the ghosts of leaves blown over moonlit snow, then I can lean back, and in a grave, almost
hesitant voice, tell the story of the young man who was
drowned in the lake that lay, a hundred years ago, in
the field beyond the coppice. A pretty story I can weave
of love unrequited, and sharp words that echo, still,
down the local lanes of legend, when men leave the inn
on cold nights, pull up their collars, and set out for home,
A story most circumstantial, of how this young man,
whose name I know, whose tortured features are clear
before me, took his terrible plunge into the dark waters.

And how, every year on March the seventeenth, or November the twenty-ninth, or whatever the date may be on which the story is being told, he is supposed to appear in my garden, for one frightful moment, lit by a horrid luminosity.

'But it's March the seventeenth, to-night.'

'To-night?'

'Yes . . . look at the calendar!'

Silence. I get up. 'It's very hot in here,' I say.

'Horribly.'

There is a sense of strain in the little room. I open the window and lean out. 'A wild night,' I say. My hand is on the switch. 'Just the sort of night . . .'

I wish I were an actor, so that I might carry through this little joke to its end. But I always break down, and laugh, and leave the switch on, so that Antinous is revealed in all his sane and exquisite beauty . . . a bright beacon against the secret, surging shadows that surround him.

2. *The light on the top of the flag-pole*

This light came next in importance to Antinous. You can call it a vulgar light, if you like. I prefer to call it a romantic one. (The boundary between vulgarity and romance, by the way, is of the very slightest — a very thin purple line, over which even the nicest of us may stray.)

I think the flag-pole light was romantic for several reasons. Firstly, because you could see it from the Great North Road, a mile away. True, you had to have good eyesight to do so, for it was only a very local star, a tiny globe of brilliance that was not at all assertive. You also had to choose your stance carefully — tiptoeing between an elm and an ash, and getting well back from the thoroughfare in order that you should not be run over by some rich merchant, cutting through the dark in his shameful chariot. Still, if you got in the right place, and looked very, very hard, you could see my light shining a mile away, like a firefly.

The light was also romantic because it was so unexpected. This statement may seem confused, but I think, with Poe, that all beauty has in it an element of the strange. And certainly, the light on top of my flag pole was strange enough to the inhabitants of Allways. It was so strange to Mr. Joy, for example, that the first time he saw it, he had the hiccups, and reeled home backwards for half a mile, and told Mrs. Joy that he would touch nothing but water till the harvest was in.

It was romantic, finally, because of the morbid attraction it had for the bats. They scooped round it, in wild circles, in such numbers that any belated maiden, passing down the lane, clutched her hair in terror. For this reason, I confess, I turn it on but seldom. For I think God made a grave mistake on the day he created bats.

3. *The Greenhouse*

I have to clutch on to my pen very firmly in order not to go completely off the deep end when I think of the excitements this light has given me. I have to push out my chin, and think of Mr. Winston Churchill, and other strong silent men — not that Mr. Winston Churchill is particularly silent — but, anyway, I have to try to be a real English gentleman, because I feel sure that a real English gentleman would not feel that he wanted to stand on his head with joy and utter shrill sounds of delight, just because he had a light in his greenhouse.

But it is not much use. For . . . oh, really . . . I mean . . . just think of it! You have walked along a dark, twisting path. The cool leaves of the elms have brushed your shoulders. You have crunched over the gravel, come suddenly upon the greenhouse; perhaps there is a faint glitter on the panes as the moon drifts, like a languid lady, from behind her silver scarves. You open the door. There is a sense of almost unbearable mystery, and a keen tang of sweetness from all the eager young life within; there is silence — and yet not quite silence — because if you hold your breath you can just hear the plants growing.

And then you switch on the light!

Instantly it is as though the curtain had risen on a very brilliant ballet. The cinerarias are poised, in dresses of fantastic blues and flaming purples . . . the cyclamen hover . . . like Sylphides waiting for the conductor's beat . . . the mimosas form a fairy trio in the wings . . . and there, poised just under the light, is my prima ballerina, a white orchid, on tiptoe, swaying in the breeze that comes from the open door.

In many ways I feel that I ought to have put the greenhouse light first in importance. It is too late now. We must go on.

4. *The light in the hall*

Now that we are back in the house we need not spend so long over each little light, or really the dawn will have come before we have had time to switch them all on. But the light in the hall is particularly fascinating, because it is placed inside an alabaster vase, of the purest Adam design. It cost the frightful sum of thirty pounds, but it is worth it. I have put it in front of an

Adam mirror, so that it shall have every opportunity of admiring its own beauty.

It is a lovely thing to see when one opens the front door and switches on the light. So elegant, after the ragged lanes . . . so chaste . . . and yet not so chaste as all that. I always feel that my Adam light is like some abnormally expensive mistress, who sits in icy allurement waiting for one to arrive, and only glows with fire when the light of her salon is switched on by her owner. Love that you turn on with the switch, love that glows always . . . is there such a difference, in the long run? I have only to write that sentence to know that it should never have been asked. But this book is an open book, and you must take the asides as they are written . . . a sign of the living breath of the writer.

5. *The light on the staircase*

This, I promise, shall be the last of the ecstasies. But if you saw this light you could not help being ecstatic about it.

It is very simple to explain. Imagine a staircase so tiny that if you stand at the bottom of it you can almost touch the top step with your hand. Half way up the staircase there is a bracket where, in the old days, a very simple kitchen lamp used to stand, sending out very simple kitchen smells. I hated the smells but I liked the bracket, and the position of the light. It used to send flattering gleams on to the old maps which surrounded it . . . casting a sunlit glow over the seventeenth-century parchments, so that one could dream that the dry charts had really come to life, that the thin lines which represented rivers (long dried up) had a prink of silver, as though ghostly waters threaded their way along them.

Just two walls, at right angles, and a bracket. So I put in a bulb, where the light had been, and waited till I found a plain print that I might stretch over it.

I waited and waited, and tried and tried, and everything was wrong. I began with flower prints, but the right one never arrived. The tulips and lad's-loves and simple phloxes looked muddy and tiresome when one saw them with the light shining through. I tried modern things . . . knowing that they would be a failure . . . sticking up little Russian mujiks, making an angry face at them and casting them down again — rather unkindly, I fear.

It was in Westminster, on an afternoon so sad that the rain on the roofs was like the tears of an old woman, and the smoke from the chimneys was as the draggled plumes of a hearse, that I suddenly met the two ladies who solved this agonizing problem for me. They were in a tiny electric shop in a back street, and the woman in the shop lit them up just as I passed the window. I stopped and stared. They were painted on a little square of parchment. They had been cut from some Lady's Album of the 'sixties. They were going for a walk, in the most fabulous and delicious attire. The wind was blowing their tresses. One of them wore a green dress and the other wore a blue. They were the loveliest ladies you have ever seen, and they rejoiced in the light. You see, if you are very beautiful, and your petticoats are white as snow and your complexion an adorable point of pink on fadeless parchment, you welcome the light, even if it shines right through you. You rejoice in it, because it gives you an opportunity to show your perpetual charms.

I bought those ladies for three shillings and sixpence.

No other ladies have ever given me anything approaching the pleasure they have given me for three shillings and sixpence, if we are talking economics.

Every night they smile me to bed, so sweetly that it is agony to part from them. For if we must speak the truth, they are night-birds, these ladies. They live with the light and for the light. In day they fade away . . . they retire . . . you don't notice them as you clatter down the stairway on your rush to the garden.

I said this was to be the last ecstasy, and I will keep my word. So we must say good night to these ladies. We rise from our chairs, kick the dying ash of the fireplace, go out into the hall, and turn on the light. It is then that the miracle happens.

A moment ago they were pale and lack-lustre, two faded ladies on a stairway, given a faint and tenuous existence by the moonlight that shines through the window of the corridor above. But now that the switch is pressed, they are alive and glowing! Miraculous roses bloom in their cheeks. The green silk and the blue silk . . . the frills and the ruches . . . the pretty painted ribbons, flying in a breeze long spent . . . all these are given once again, a happy, buoyant life.

Slowly I walk up the tiny stairway. Ten steps in all. At the fifth step I pause. My face is only a few inches from the faces of the little painted ladies. I smile at them. They smile at me. The ribbons blow. The silks, I swear, are fluttering. Their feet, pointed so exquisitely from the caressing laces, seem longing to dance out of the frame, to dance up my staircase, into my room, out again, and then into the moonlight, with many a twist and turn and sigh of faded silk . . . as long as the light shall last.

As long as the light shall last! Aye . . . there's the rub. For I, who brought them from the darkness must send them back again . . . back into the shadows where their silks no longer glow, and the roses die from their cheeks. Yes . . . they must go back, no longer giving themselves these airs of life. They must return to the Victorian shadows where they belong. I must turn out the light.

It is an agonizing business, this turning out of the light. As my hand touches the switch, they seem to plead with me. 'See . . . we are so pretty . . . our dresses are so gay . . . the feathers in our bonnets were dyed but yesterday, . . . our lips are red as red . . . may we not have a moment longer?' I stand and stare at them. I wish they would dance out of their frame, for ever, and leave me at peace, those painted ladies. I wish I might turn out the light on a sheet of blank paper. But no . . . they stay there entreating. They never move. And in the end, I tell myself not to be a damned fool, and I turn out the light.

But always, I feel like a murderer.

CHAPTER XX

WOMEN ABOUT THE HOUSE

AND now, a man might say, the tale is told. There is nothing more to be said. For we have seen, stage by stage, how the cottage was made clean and white; how the new windows let in the air of heaven, how the spirit of the garden flowed through it, how it was warmed and lit. What more can there be to write about?

The average woman will agree that with me there can be a great deal more to write about. For these things which we have recorded are only the foundations of the story. They are merely the background against which the principal drama moves — the drama of 'managing the house.' It is very much easier, if you can afford it, to make structural alterations, even if they are extremely elaborate, than to achieve domestic peace and happiness, to manage to have good food, to avoid 'rows,' to obtain cleanliness without feeling that you dare not flick any ash on the carpet.

You may say that all these things are only the result of being lucky enough to have a clever housekeeper. But really it isn't quite as simple as that. There are many women who have excellent housekeepers, whose lives, none the less, are a desolation of muddle and worry.

In order not to be unjust, let me take, as an object of criticism, Mrs. M., for she is really a very efficient woman. And yet . . .

We will let her speak for herself. We will go to lunch with her, as I did, not long since.

§ 11

The lunch was on Palm Sunday.

Mrs. M. always goes to church on festival days. She goes in order to count the flowers she has given, so that she may be sure the vicar has not kept any of them back for his own drawing-room, instead of grouping them round the pulpit. Why she should do this, I cannot imagine, because the vicar has never shown any inclination towards this nefarious practice — indeed, his own garden is as bare as a desert on the Saturday evenings before such events. Nevertheless, Mrs. M. always goes to church early when she has given flowers.

You can see her sitting in her pew, her eyes darting from pot to pot. 'I gave seven cinerarias,' she is muttering. 'I only see six.'

I have observed her, on certain occasions, leave her pew, before the service begins, and pretend to go over to borrow a Prayer Book from Mrs. Joy, who sits on the other side of the church, in order that she may see if she can trace the seventh cineraria. It is usually lurking at the steps of the pulpit. Mrs. M. smiles at it, nods, forgets to borrow the Prayer Book from Mrs. Joy, and returns to her pew leaving us all, I fear, a little distracted.

The object of my lunch with Mrs. M. was to help her choose things for a jumble sale, because she was having her annual tidy-up. However, there was also an ulterior motive behind the invitation.

'It will do you good to see how a *woman* keeps her house in order, for a change,' she observed.

I humbly agreed that it would do me a lot of good, and accepted. I also went to church, because the sermon would obviously be an excellent topic of conversation if there were any awkward silences at lunch.

Mrs. M. sits just behind me. She has quite a pretty contralto and she is not unmusical. But unfortunately, she invariably scorns the tune and insists upon singing 'parts.'

The result is highly disturbing to the humble person, who, like myself, tries to sing the tune without feeling too self-conscious about it. The little organ begins the *Te Deum*. We stand up. I prepare a timid A natural, on which the chant opens. But Mrs. M., a second before I have given out my A, sings a ferocious D. I descend in sympathy, but she promptly rises. I come down again, trying to meet her half-way, because when anybody is singing a very loud second behind you, your voice wobbles and eventually falls to their pitch. But no sooner have I got to Mrs. M.'s D than she has leaped to my A natural. However pleasing the harmonics may, or may not, be, this practice is not conducive to a state of religious fervour.

§ I I I

We had roast beef for lunch, and Yorkshire pudding, and lovely baked potatoes which were *all* brown, all over, like a biscuit. Usually there is only one really brown, hard potato in the dish, so that one doesn't know whether to be greedy, and take it — pretending airily that one thinks it is just like all the other potatoes — or whether to be polite and pass it by. But at Mrs. M.'s, all the potatoes were brown, so this problem did not arise.

There was also some beautiful cooked celery, covered with a white sauce.

'Out of the garden,' said Mrs. M., with a bright smile, as I took some of the celery.

I smiled back. But as I lifted the celery on to my plate, the smile faded, for I noticed that the celery looked slightly darker than ordinary fresh celery. It looked indeed, exactly like a certain tinned variety which I used myself. I do not like many things out of tins, but there is an English firm which sells wonderful tinned celery, green peas and raspberries. And there are some tinned American soups which are delicious.

Well — I should soon know. I wound my fork round the celery. Before eating it I would give Mrs. M. one more chance.

'Out of the garden?' I repeated innocently.

But Mrs. M. flushed slightly. She did not repeat the assertion in so many words, but she said, sharply, 'I always wonder why you find it so difficult to grow celery.'

That settled it. I devoured a piece of celery.

Tinned!

There was absolutely no question about it. The celery mind you, was grand — much better than the average fresh celery. But it happened to have come out of a tin. I felt very angry with Mrs. M. for telling such fibs. I said acidly:

'Your cook always does these things so well.'

'My cook has gone, if you're referring to Daisy.'

'Gone? But you had her only about six months.'

Mrs. M. snorted. 'She was impossible!'

'But how?'

Mrs. M. paused a moment, as though wondering

whether she could take me into her confidence. 'It was a question of the hours she used to come in at night. Ten-thirty . . . eleven . . . sometimes nearly midnight!'

I nodded sympathetically. 'I suppose she used to make a fiendish noise, and wake you up.'

'On the contrary, she was so quiet that I had to sit up for her, or I should have never known when she came in.'

'But, in that case what did it matter?'

'What did it *matter?* Really! I can't have my girls staying out all night.'

'But she didn't stay out all night.'

'Well, till midnight, then. It's the same thing in the country.'

'But why not, Mrs. M.?'

I was not trying to embarrass poor Mrs. M. And it was a full minute before I realized what she meant. 'Certain' things, it appeared, might be happening to Daisy in her nocturnal prowls. That was the trouble.

I protested against this suggestion. 'She was *hideous*, Mrs. M. Very fat, and shortsighted, and a revolting complexion. . . .'

'What has that got to do with it?' inquired Mrs. M., coldly.

Now that she asked the question, I supposed that it really had very little to do with it, judging from the ghoulish girls who apparently rouse passion in some men's hearts. Yet, I was still unsatisfied as to Mrs. M.'s explanation.

'But surely, Mrs. M., if Daisy wanted to be led astray, she could be led astray just as well between the hours of eight and ten, as between the hours of ten and midnight.'

'That's beside the point.'

'On the contrary, it *is* the point, the whole point, and nothing but the point. You can't keep servants because. . . .'

'Ssh!'

The door opened and the housemaid appeared with the apple tart. For two minutes we both made feverish remarks about the cream and crust and how things were still going down. As soon as the door closed, I resumed:

'Because you don't allow them any liberty. You *say* it's because you have to look after their morals. . . .'

'It is.'

'But if you paused to think for one minute you'd realize that you're not affecting their morals one way or the other.'

'I may be old-fashioned, but. . . .'

'Well, Mrs. M.,' I said, somewhat hotly, 'I think that in this matter it *is* a little old-fashioned to . . .'

'In that case we won't discuss the matter.'

We finished our apple tart in silence. I was burning with the wrongs of the dismissed Daisy. It seems a small matter, but I happen to feel deeply about it. Domestic servants, as a general rule, lead lives of unspeakable drudgery. They only get one night off — or possibly two — a week. What conceivable difference can it make to their employer if they come in at ten, or twelve, or six o'clock in the morning, provided that they do their work? If they are of the sort that 'goes wrong,' they most assuredly *will* 'go wrong,' at whatever hour they come in.

That is one of the charges I would bring against many women who run houses. That is why I am writing about this lunch with Mrs. M., because she is about to give us another very flagrant example of feminine sin.

§ I V

But first . . . the celery.

In order to reach the hay-loft, where the objects for the jumble sale were accumulated we had to pass along a little brick pathway that led past the kitchen door, into a yard.

When we had finished our coffee, we went through the French windows, across the lawn, and made for this path. As we neared the kitchen door there were loud sounds of washing up, accompanied by hymns. I saw Mrs. M. frown. She intensely dislikes these domestic noises. She has an amazingly keen ear for them, and can hear remarks which no ordinary woman could possibly hear, provided that these remarks are made in the kitchen.

There was a feeling of thunder in the air, although it was early spring. Our footsteps echoed hollowly over the pavement. And just as we came past the kitchen door, out bustled the new cook, a pleasant, robust-looking creature of about fifty. She was walking so quickly that she collided with Mrs. M., and dropped something which she was carrying in her hand.

'Oh!' said the cook, in one tone of voice.

'Oh!' said Mrs. M. in another tone.

'Oh!' said I, in yet another.

And the 'something' rolled over and over the pavement with a loud, clattering noise, eventually coming to rest at the foot of the dustbin to which the cook had been bearing it.

The 'something' was an empty tin of Blank's celery. It lay there, glistening in the sunlight, with the title shining out in terrible and accusing clarity: *'Blank's Superfine Hearts of Celery.'*

Time stopped.

How it ever started again, I do not know. But eventually our legs moved forward once more, our lips formed aimless sentences, the attic stairs were climbed, and we found ourselves in the jumble saleroom. But it was a long time before we could really get down to business. We were both too shattered.

It says much for the sterling character of Mrs. M. that she was able in the next half hour to give a positively firework-like display of the other feminine vice to which I previously alluded — the vice of hoarding.

§ v

It began with a photograph, which was lying partly hidden under a piece of old mink. I picked it up, and looked at it.

The photograph portrayed a heavily-moustached gentleman staring with a look of grave suspicion at a Grecian urn.

'Who is this?'

'That? Oh — that is my Uncle Frederick.'

I looked at Uncle Frederick. It seemed terrible that

he had been forced to stare for all those years at that urn. Could he not have a little excitement, and go to the jumble sale?

'I think somebody might buy it for the frame,' I suggested tentatively.

Mrs. M. spoke very sharply. 'You don't imagine I'm going to send *that* to the sale?'

'Well . . . I suppose it is a bit . . .'

'Really!' She rose from her knees and snatched the photograph from me. 'With all its associations!'

'What associations?' I asked this question because I knew that Uncle Frederick had died of apoplexy at the funeral of Queen Victoria. We had often been told this, by Mrs. M. It seemed, somehow, to reflect a certain grandeur upon her. I thought that Mrs. M. might be able to give me a few historical details.

'Associations,' Mrs. M. repeated loftily.

'But you were only a little girl . . .'

'And I was taught to *respect* my relations.'

'Well, I don't think Uncle Frederick would be particularly honoured to be lying in the attic under a piece of old mink, if it comes to that.'

It was lucky I mentioned the mink, because the conversation was again becoming a little heated.

Mrs. M. took up the mink and shook it violently in her irritation. A cloud of dust came out of it. We both squeezed the outside of our noses to stop ourselves from sneezing.

'I must have this cleaned,' said Mrs. M.

'Is there time, before the sale?'

'And why should I send *this* to the sale?'

'But it's quite good enough, Mrs. M.'

'Good *enough*?' she shook out the mink once more. And this time she could not squeeze her nose quickly enough to stop herself from sneezing. When she had finished, she said, 'It's far *too* good.' She sneezed again. 'It's bound to "come in," some day.'

I had been waiting for her to say that. All over England there are dusty hoards in cupboards which ought long ago to have been destroyed — old pieces of material; odd shoes, worn-out tennis racquets, balls that have long ceased to bounce, ornament boxes, keys that fit nothing — all kept because they may 'come in.'

That phrase gives me terrible visions. I cannot help interpreting it literally. I see myself sitting in an empty room. There is a dull scratching on the door. Slowly the door opens, and the mink 'comes in.' It stalks across the room, sending out clouds of dust. And just before it springs upon me, I sneeze and wake up.

Often these objects are kept for sentimental reasons. But usually the sentiment has long faded.

Mrs. M. pointed to a little cluster of ebony elephants in a corner. They were one of those frightful 'families' of elephants, the biggest about five inches high, and the baby being the size of a pea. You are supposed to think it is terribly amusing to have a baby elephant the size of a pea. Housemaids, who have to dust it, do not always see the joke.

'Those elephants,' said Mrs. M.

'Yes,' I could not decide whether she wanted me to say how loathsome they were, or whether I ought to suggest that they would 'come in.'

'My cousin in India sent them to me — Colonel Waters-Thompson — you remember?'

I not only remembered him, but I also recalled that Mrs. M. heartily detested him.

'Then let's send them to the sale at once,' I suggested brightly.

'But supposing he comes home on leave, and comes up here, and asks to see them?'

'You could say they'd all gone out for the day.'

Mrs. M. projected her rabbit's teeth at a certain angle which warned me that she was not amused.

'I happen to be related to him,' she said.

I was growing hot and tired and impatient.

'But you're not related to the elephants, Mrs. M.'

Which finished it. We descended from the attic, in silence, having chosen nothing at all for the jumble sale. I tried to make up for my abominable rudeness by sending Mrs. M. a huge sack of gladioli bulbs. But it was a long time before we were really friends again.

In the end, she sent the mink to the sale. It was bought by Mrs. Joy for five shillings. She wears it round her neck, on cold Sundays, in church. It becomes her very well. And often I have looked out of the corner of my eye, during the Psalms, and seen Mrs. M. glaring with a very unchristian expression at Mrs. Joy and her mink, saying to herself, 'It *would* have come in, after all.'

§ VI

If I did not know better, and had read the foregoing pages, I should have formed a very unfavourable opinion of myself. It seems that I am always grousing about the follies of 'women about the house.' I can't think why. I probably realize their problems, as sympathetically as most men.

Oh yes — there are a hundred and one little irritations in running a house, and perhaps it is because women have to face them, day in and day out, that they occasionally lose their sense of proportion — grow angry with young servants who are full of life and want to stay out till all hours of the morning. Poor dears: *they* can't stay out till all hours of the morning, themselves. Their families have too many insistent claims on them.

One day I want to write a book which shall show something of the heroism of the average ordinary woman. A heroism that most men do not even suspect, or, if they sense it vaguely, take it for granted.

One very small example will suffice to show you the sort of book I want to write. And then this sentimental homily can be finished. The example is the 'family meal.'

Family meals are not, in themselves, inspiring things. But have you ever thought that they might be rather terrible, rather frightening, if it weren't that the women make them otherwise? There might come moments when sons and fathers and daughters and wives suddenly paused, and set down their glasses, and stared about them, in a sort of horror, saying, 'Who are these people? These men, and women, and children? Why are they sitting here? What have they to do with *me?* What is it all about?'

Those moments do come, even in the best regulated families. But somehow, by some miracle, the quiet woman who is sitting at the end of the table saves the situation. She herself is an entity — don't forget that — she herself has her dreams and her moods, her frets and her aches. But she sets them aside.

She says:

'I saw Miss Thompson this afternoon. Her sister is going to get a caravan.'

One son — the clever one — sniffs contemptuously. What does he care about Miss Thompson, or her caravan? However, the subject has been introduced, and he is led subtly away from his brooding on a more dangerous subject — a subject which *she* noticed, and understood, and feared.

The other son — the dull, elder one — also sniffs contemptuously. Really, mother and her old Miss Thompson, what the devil is there in that? All the same, a caravan would be fun. It might be grand in a caravan. Before he knows what he is about, his mind is off, over the hills, and the smoke of gipsy meals is assailing his nostrils.

'What *can* she see in that old Miss Thompson?' thinks the father, wearily. Yet for him, too, there is a momentary respite from the thoughts that were torturing him. If only he had sold, instead of buying! If only he had bought instead of selling! Well, if things go on like this, they'll be lucky if they have even a caravan between them.

They don't answer the quiet woman who is sitting at the head of the table. They say 'Oh' or 'really,' or other words that cost nothing. But somehow the atmosphere is changed.

And she? Does she care about Miss Thompson and her caravan? Does she? You know that she cares not at all. That this little sentence is only one tiny symbol of the constant, tireless effort she makes, all her life, to keep the family a going concern, to keep its members happy, holding up their heads, each fulfilling his separate purpose — a purpose, generally, far higher in her imagination than it will ever be in reality.

No. She does not care about Miss Thompson and her caravan. And as she sits there, in the fading light, looking at the faces of her family, the man she loved, the children she bore him, she wonders if it is all worth while. For a brief terrible moment the longings which for years she had been suppressing descend upon her, tearing her with eager talons.

'If only . . .' she cries to herself. 'If only . . . .'

But she never finishes the sentence. It might be dangerous for her.

It would certainly be dangerous for me.

CHAPTER XXI

SWEETS TO THE SWEET

ADVENTURES were always happening at Allways. And the last adventure of all was, in some ways, the most exciting.

You remember the little alcove we found in the Garden Room, with the White Lady walled up in it? Well, that was a thrill, if you like. But the last thrill was greater.

It happened one day when Undine Wilkins came for sherry. Undine never drinks cocktails. There is nothing olde worlde about them, you see. But she drinks quantities of sherry, and is fortunately quite unaware of the difference between Amontillado 1900 and Smith's Best Cooking, 1933. Whichever she gets, she quivers her nostrils, and half closes her eyes and savours the sherry, murmuring 'Ah!' A quite sincere 'Ah!' I may say, even if it is a quite sour sherry.

While we were drinking our sherry, we talked about ghosts. Undine, I need hardly mention, was 'psychic.' She saw auras. At least she told us she did, and nobody except Mrs. M. ever contradicted her. She also heard strange sounds at night — hissing sounds in the lane outside her cottage. Mrs. M. said the sounds came from Mrs. Joy's stray geese, but Undine knew better.

Anyway, after talking about ghosts for some time, Undine said that she should like to go upstairs and 'Sense the atmosphere.' At first I wondered if this was a

Tudor way of saying that she would like to wash her hands. But no . . . she really did wish to sense the atmosphere. And so we prowled about upstairs, in and out of the little bedrooms, while she walked in front, breathing very heavily.

Nothing happened, and we were both a little disappointed.

It was just as we were about to come downstairs again that Undine suddenly stopped, like a pointer.

'What is in that cupboard?' she hissed.

'Which cupboard?'

'There! In that corner!' She darted out an accusing finger at the corner of the room.

'Good Lord!' I stepped up to it. 'I didn't even know there was a cupboard there.'

I knelt down. It was a very tiny cupboard, which had been so often whitewashed over that it was almost indistinguishable from the wall. The handle had long ago been torn off, or worn away. The woodwork had been painted many times, and the paint had mingled with the whitewash, so that it would need a knife to prise it open.

'It's pretty well glued up.'

'There is something in it,' breathed Undine.

I looked round and stared at her. She spoke with such conviction that for a moment I almost believed her.

'What sort of thing?'

'I don't know. I can only . . . I can only . . . sense it.'

I paused. It would be a great bore to make an ugly patch on the wall by tearing open the door and breaking the paint. On the other hand, there *might* be something in it. The spirit of adventure seized me. I felt in my pocket for a knife. Good! Here it was. I took out the knife, ran it down the edges of the cupboard, inserted the blade, prised it very gently. There was a sudden creak, and the door flew open.

Before I knew what had happened, Undine had rushed over like a whirlwind, and thrust her arm into the cupboard. She drew it out quickly again, bearing with it a white object which I could not see clearly, because she instantly hugged it in her arms.

'Oh!' she screamed . . . 'Oh! Oh! *Oh!*'

'What's happened? What is it? Have you been bitten?'

'*Oh!*' cried Undine again, a little less shrilly.

'But what is it? What *is* it?'

'A Booke,' she breathed. I swear she made it sound like that. It *was* a book, a very old book, bound in yellow parchment. But only Undine could have given it such an ultra-Tudor intonation.

'Where? How? Let me *see* . . . .'

'It was in there,' she gasped, pointing to the hole in the wall, but keeping a tight hold of the book, which I was longing to seize from her.

I lit a match and flashed it into the cupboard. It revealed nothing but a tiny alcove, about three feet deep. I put in my hand and tapped the walls. They were quite solid. It was obvious that the Booke which Undine was clasping was the only discovery we were going to make. So I turned to her.

'What . . .' I began.

'Listen!' She raised a long, tapering finger on which an immense moonstone glistened, commanding silence.

With her other hand she smoothed out the dusty parchment that was lying on her lap, and read in a voice that
trembled, but was clear; the following receipt:—

'*To make Sugar plate to print.* In mouls or to make any
Artificial Frutes or Muscardine comfits.

'Take a small quantity of gum dragaunt, and lay it in
steep in rosewater till it is desolved into a gelly, then
strain it through a Cloth and beat it in a morter, till it
looks very white, then put some searced sugar into it,
and beat together, & when you have beaten it wi^th so
much searced sugar, y^t it is so stif, y^t you may take
it out of yoe Morter, take it forth and work it into a stif
paste wth searsed sugar, so you may print it in yo^e mouls
or use it otherwise, as you pleased.'

§ 11

This is a true story. And because it is true, it will
probably sound false. Oscar Wilde once said, 'Nothing
looks so like innocence as an indiscretion.' In the same
way, nothing sounds so like a lie as the truth.

Yet we *did* discover that book in that cupboard. And
if anybody doubts it, I will show it to him, in its faded
parchment, with the title page-half eaten away by rats:

A

RECEIPT BOOK

OF

COOCKERY.

1698

Some of the recipes are a good deal older than 1698, as Undine and I discovered.

Eagerly we leant over that book, in the fading light — a golden October sunset that flooded in on the yellow parchment — yellow to yellow, with the grave black letters dancing before our eyes, as though they were overjoyed to be read again, after two hundred and fifty years of neglect. And as we turned the pages it seemed that there was a scent in the old room of ghostly sweetmeats; there drifted back to us the perfume of curious country wines, the aroma of forgotten preserves, the bitter-sweet flavour of kitchens which have long crumbled into dust.

Why — the very titles were dripping with poetry, like jars of country wine that cannot contain their sweetness. Listen!

To Preserve Quinces Red or White.

To Make Paste or Apricocks Very Goode.

To Make Red Muscardine Comfits.

To Make Slipcoat Chees. The Lady Bray's Recipe.

To Dry All Manner of Green Ploms.

To Boile Sugar to a Thine Sirrup.

To Know When Sugar is Boiled to a Manus Christie Heighte.[1]

To Make Quodeny of any Kind of Plumes.

And then, there were other recipes — secret recipes — a page of very faded print headed Aqua Mirabilis, which made me feel like an alchemist who at last has discovered the philtre of immortality.

I will skip these ecstasies, and draw a veil over the

---

[1] If some kind reader would interpret this archaic sentence, I should be deeply interested.

unfortunate 'difference' which arose between **Undine** and myself over this book. She said that as she had 'sensed' it, the book belonged, by rights, to her. I differed. The result, in the long run, was eminently satisfactory to both parties. I spread the fame of Undine's psychic powers all over Allways, and sent her a copy of the book, beautifully typed, and accompanied by a dozen really good Amontillado. I also asked her, on many occasions, to come and taste the recipes at dinner. She came, bless her heart. And whether they were good or bad, she adored them.

Here are a few of the recipes for which I can vouch by personal experience.

§ I I I

There are three recipes for Cowslip wine. Each time the word cowslip is spelt in a different way. Thus:—

> Cowslep
> Couslepe
> Couslip

Of these, the first recipe is the best. I copy it below, and will add that when we gave it to the men who were digging out the new pond last spring, two of them fell into the pond, and all of their wives complained to me, 'which pleased me mightily,' as Pepys might say. Here it is:

'*To Make Cowslep Wine. Martha Benthall.* Take 7 gallons of water put in as much sugar as w^{ll} make it so strong as it w^{ll} bear an Egg, set it on ye fire till it w^ll be clear that no Scum w^ll arise, so let it stand untel it be but blood warm, so poure it on 2 Pecks of couslep pips, then put in 4 Lemons cut peell and all in, then let it stand wth a quarter or half of a pint of good lite yest fo^r to work, then let it stand a day and a night, then strain out the Cowleps, then put ye Lemons into ye barrell, then let it stand about 2 weeks before you bottle it.'

§ I V

Here is a recipe for making snuff. If you have never taken snuff there is obviously something lacking in your life. The first time I ever had it was at Trinity College, Cambridge, where I once dined at the High Table with the dons, for some obscure reason which neither I nor the dons appeared to have grasped. At this college they hand round a large and most exquisite early Georgian snuff-box, while you are having your port in the Combination Room. The silver is so brightly polished that you can see all the windows latticed in silver, and your own face reflected, like a lovely pink balloon, as you bend over to take your snuff. There are five sorts . . . or is it six? I forget. But I remember that they are graded very delicately, in varying degrees of fineness.

I always forget if a gentleman sneezes or doesn't sneeze when he takes snuff. There is a very definite rule about it. As I always sneeze, I assume that gentlemen do not.

Here is the recipe for Snuffe:—

'*To Make Snuffe*. Take 2 Ounces of bestt Tobacco 2

Nutmegs of Sweett marjorum Rosemary Germandor Bittony & Bassilli thimes one handfulle pound all these welle together & pouder them very fine & youse it for snuffe.'

§ v

However, these recipes are a little esoteric for the average housewife. She would be more interested in a recipe dated 1752, 'To Make Blummonge' . . . . A lovely word, Blummonge, which makes one think of a baby, bubbling out its lips rather angrily, as it bangs a petulant spoon against its sillabub. But an even lovelier word is 'Marchpane,' for which I will certainly give you the recipe.

Why do we insist upon calling Marchpane 'Marzipan'? Marzipan is a bastard Teutonic innovation. It is the sort of word that a fanatic spits out at his troops, when urging them on to further follies. Cakes of marzipan, I feel, have evil omens printed on their bottoms. But Marchpane . . . ah! that is cool and delicious. A fragrant word, pastoral and English, in the best sense of the word 'English,' recalling the days when England was tiny, and young and infinitely lovable. Here is the recipe:—

'*To Make Marchpane Paste.* Take a pound of Almonds & blanch them, and beat them to mash in a Morter, then put half a pound of sugar to them, and beat them together an houre, and it w^ll be in a paste, and if you see your paste beat Oylie put into it a little Rose water, and beat it together and that w^ll take away the Oylinefs

276

from it, and so you may print it in your moulds, make a Machpane wth it, or use it otherwise as you please.'

I can vouch for that recipe. It makes the best march-pane you ever tasted. I gave a supply of it to a very charming American girl only six months ago, to use on her wedding cake. She is not yet divorced. So you see that it must have magic qualities.

§ VI

As I wander through this Receipt book it becomes more and more evident that I shall have to publish it, one day, in its entirety, with a preface of enchanting prose, that will drift as lightly and as savourously as the scent of roast meats from the kitchen when the door is open on winter nights, and hunger is gripping you. Yes, that will be a happy task! But it would be wicked to make you wait so long for some of the other recipes. I will choose them quickly, before I relent.

What about *Mifs Leblanc's Receit to Hew Carp?* Would you like that? Not very much, I imagine. Apart from the fact that neither you nor I have the faintest idea how, or why, you should 'hew' carp, apart from the fact that it suggests a deadly female poised, at twilight, with a hatchet, over an enormous and rather bloody fish; apart from the fact that we know, by instinct, that carp is uneatable; apart from all these facts, there is that dreadful feeling about Mifs Leblanc. Whenever I read F's for S's, in old books, whenever I read, in fact, about misses who are spelt Mifses, I always feel that these ladies are fizzing, protruding their rather prominent teeth and . . . well . . . fizzing. And I do not want anybody to fizz over my carp. So we will leave this recipe, and give you three other recipes — two of which I can recommend, and another which I can't. Here are the two which I can recommend.

'*To Stew a Rabit or a Hear — from Ann Bruton.* Quarter him and wash him and of nutmeg Clover Mace Cinaman and pepper of each a small quantity & mix it wth salt y^n take a small quantity of pot time and marjorum & strip & shed y^m mix ye spice and herbs together and so season ye rabit wth it. There must be a small quantity of water in ye stewing as mich as will cover ye botom of ye pot or something more it must stew gently for an hour and a half & before you take it off ye fire you must put in a good peice of buttor and shake it about if you stew a Hear 2 or 3 hours it w^{ll} be little enough.'

If you cook a rabbit in this way, it tastes more delicious than chicken.

Here is the other recommended recipe.

'*Scotch Collops.* Take Veal and cut it thine pieces then take some sweet herbs minse them very small wth Clove Mace & Nutmegs pounded wth a little Salt then put it on Your Veale Fry it in Butter, make some strong broth, put in Mushromes, Anchovie & Clarrit & pickled Oysters & butter make Veal bales & Frey them broune, take ye Yolke of 2 or 3 Eges then dip ye Clary in it, then Frye it Broune then Slise some Baken thin & Fry it, then Lay it on Your Meat.'

I might have chosen more sensational recipes, but I wanted you to feel that this book had *some* utilitarian value, and was not merely a wild egotistical meandering, shot through with occasional flashes of poetry and laughter. For the sensation-monger I append the final recipe, which is written across two pages, and emblazoned with such a fury of whirling capitals that even the centuries cannot dim the shock it gives you. Thus:

'*Mad Dog.* Doctʳ Mead's Remedy for the Bite of a mad Dog.

Let the Patient be blooded at the Arm 9 or 10 Ounces. Take of the Herb called in Latin Lichen Cinerieus Terrestris, in English, Ash-colour'd Ground Liverwort, clean'd dry'd and powder'd, half an Ounce.

Of black Pepper powder'd, two Drachms.

Mix these well together, and divide the Powder into four Doses, one of which must be taken every Morning, fasting for four mornings succefsively, in half a Pint of Cow's Milk warm: after these four Doses are taken, the Patient must go into the Cold Bath, or a cold Spring or River, every morning fasting, for a month; he must be dipt all over, but not stay in (with his Head above water) longer than half a Minute, if the Water be very cold: After this he must go in three times a Week for a Fort-night longer.

The Lichan is a very comõn Herb and grows generally in sandy and barren Soils all over England. The right time to gather it is in the Months of October or November.

The Doctʳ says in the Experience of above thirty Years, upon more than 500 Patients he has never known the above Remedy to fail of succefs: He says That the sooner the Medicine is taken after the Bite, the better, though he had often found it to answer, though not taken 'till a Fortnight, or even a longer time after it.'

'The sooner the medicine is taken after the bite,' you see, 'the better.'

And the sooner I say good-bye, the better. For we have lingered long enough.

CHAPTER XXII

GOOD-BYE

IN my bedroom there is a white wall, sloping and irregular, where one day there will be a window. I do not know when it shall be built, because this is the window through which I wish to take my last look at the fields and trees of Allways. It may be soon, or it may be late . . . I don't know. I believe one has an instinct in these things, like the animals, when they creep away to the most silent parts of the wood, and lie down because they know that there is a chill in the wind which they have never felt before.

I do not think that it is morbid to wish to die in a beloved place. A story must have an ending, and it is good that the ending should be beautiful, and that this body of ours which, in life has been twisted to such grotesque uses, which has gestured so pitifully, run in so many races, lain in so many rooms, suffered such pain, and inflicted it, been vibrant with glory and dull with shame . . . it is good that this body should in its last moment know peace and fall with grace . . . that the last leaf should drift down to soil that it loves rather than be torn by the winds and sent flying along cold and hostile skies.

And so one day I shall send for the carpenter — he is a young man now but perhaps, by then, he may be old, or perhaps not so old, and I shall show him the wall where the vine and the lilac and the white rose are planted, and shall point to the part of the thatch where the window is to be made. And then we shall go up to my room. . . .

'If you put the window here I shall be able to see the vine while I am lying in bed. . . .'

'Yes sir — you always thought of having a window here.'

'Yes — I always thought of it — but I did not feel the time had come, till now. So will you work quickly please?'

§ 11

And they will come, and lay their sheets on the floor, and the plaster will fall. There will be a rending of wood and a rush of air and then, for the first time, I shall be able to look through my wall.

Ah! That's good. I have planted well. The white plumes of the lilac are now tall enough to nod their heads at me as I sit down and watch the plasterers at work. Perhaps I shall see the lilacs again . . . perhaps not; what matter? I have seen them once. They will never be forgotten, now, as they pay me their silver obeisance against the blue skies of spring. And see . . . that vine . . . we could trail it round and round the window till it is as giddy as the grapes it may never form for me And there is a rose — a very humble white rose that I love so much that it hurts me as if it plunged its thorns into my heart . . . even the rose is on tiptoe now, and if I reach up, up . . . a little higher . . . I can see her, quite easily.

The plasterers will work on and I shall leave them, because the evening is growing cold, and I shall wander out into the garden, a little glumly. God . . . what a sentimental old fool! What a disgusting orgy of self-indulgence and self-pity! I shall kick a pebble out of my way, and get a twinge of rheumatism for my pains.

'It won't be a bit like that,' I shall mutter to myself. 'And even if it is, it's early days to think of it.' And I shall brace myself up, and suffer another twinge of rheumatism. But I shall defeat it, and call to my aid the last arguments of cynicism which, in youth, were always so readily on tap when the great and tragic facts of life loomed, like erring spectres, out of the still distant darkness. Yes, I shall invoke these tawdry arguments, borrowing for the last time the phrases of my youth . . .

'It'll be in a taxi . . . or a Tube . . . or at the club . . . when you have dined too well . . . or when that fool, . . . what is his name? . . . even my memory's going . . . when that fool has been boring everybody to death . . . that's what you'll die of . . . being bored to death. . . .'

And I shall laugh, and laugh again, all alone, in a deserted garden. But when I have finished laughing, I shall shudder, because the echo will be ugly. It will not be in tune with the sweet night wind. And as I look up, the new window will be staring at me, reproachfully, as though it were staring into my heart.

§ III

Well, my friend, I have done laughing. And mocking and dreaming. And I have finished putting my hand over the dream as though it were a white butterfly that would dance out of the window before I had time to see it . . . or rather, before *you* had time to see it . . . for there are dreams we share, and dreams we keep to ourselves . . . and it is my eternal problem that I do not know to what extent I may trust you with my dreams.

Therefore I would ask you to forget the empty laugh of the old man who prophesied death in strange fashions and in alien places. For it will not be like that. It cannot be like that.

For I know that wherever I die, in the last moment, my spirit will fly to that white room over the quiet fields. I may die in poverty or in exile, but no man will be able to bar me from this place which I have loved and which is mine for always. It may be in some shabby hotel bedroom, in some southern country . . . with a concierge knocking at the door, and peering in through the thickening dusk, to see if the old Englishman, who lives there alone, is still alive. Or in a café, when suddenly I see the mirrors darken before me, and the noise of the orchestra is blown darkly away by the last gusts, as the wind blows away the howling of a dog on winter nights. Or at sea, when the waves leap up for the last time, and remain stiff and frozen, while the immense sky closes in, with no star to give me light.

But wherever the hand of Death may seize me, near or far, rich or poor, alone or in a gay company, I shall by BEVERLEY NICHOLS

Down the Garden Path

'A delicious book . . . he has
taken pure wit for his material.'
JAMES AGATE in the *Daily Express*

> 'This most graceful and whim-
> sical of garden books.' *Country
> Life*

'Mr. Beverley Nichols's new book
must surely rank as the best of his
three excursions into autobio-
graphy. He is at his best with
flowers and his best is charming.'
GERALD BULLETT in the *Observer*

> 'Mr. Nichols has produced a
> book about his garden in Hunting-
> donshire that will bring delight to
> the reader who has never so much
> as grown mustard and cress in a
> window box.' *The Church Times*

'When you have laughed yourself
silly at his delectable wit you can
go into the garden feeling that you
have learnt a lot.' CECIL ROBERTS
in *The Sphere*

> ILLUSTRATED BY REX
> WHISTLER 7s. 6d. net

JONATHAN CAPE

escape him. I shall escape him utterly. Over sea and forest and city, in that strange, tortured moment of consummation which all must know, I shall fly . . . and I shall get there before Death. Yes . . . I shall be in the white room over the quiet fields, even if it is only for the last second, for the last 'look round.'